Decoding the TOEFL® iBT

Actual Test

SPEAKING 2

INTRODUCTION

For many learners of English, the TOEFL® iBT will be the most important standardized test they ever take. Unfortunately for a large number of these individuals, the material covered on the TOEFL® iBT remains a mystery to them, so they are unable to do well on the test. We hope that by using the *Decoding the TOEFL® iBT* series, individuals who take the TOEFL® iBT will be able to excel on the test and, in the process of using the book, may unravel the mysteries of the test and therefore make the material covered on the TOEFL® iBT more familiar to themselves.

The TOEFL® iBT covers the four main skills that a person must learn when studying any foreign language: reading, listening, speaking, and writing. The *Decoding the TOEFL® iBT* series contains books that cover all four of these skills. The *Decoding the TOEFL® iBT* series contains books with three separate levels for all four of the topics, and it also contains *Decoding the TOEFL® iBT Actual Test* books. These books contain several actual tests that learners can utilize to help them become better prepared to take the TOEFL® iBT. This book, *Decoding the TOEFL® iBT Actual Test Speaking 2*, covers the speaking aspect of the test and includes both independent and integrated tasks that are arranged in the same format as the TOEFL® iBT. Finally, the TOEFL® iBT underwent a number of changes in August 2019. This book—and the others in the series—takes those changes into account and incorporates them in the texts and questions, so readers of this second edition can be assured that they have up-to-date knowledge of the test.

Decoding the TOEFL® iBT Actual Test Speaking 2 can be used by learners who are taking classes and also by individuals who are studying by themselves. It contains a total of twenty full-length speaking actual tests. Each actual test contains one independent task (question 1) and three integrated tasks (questions 2-4). All of the passages, conversations, and lectures that are used in the tasks are the same length and have the same difficulty levels as those found on the TOEFL® iBT. Individuals who use *Decoding the TOEFL® iBT Actual Test Speaking 2* will therefore be able to prepare themselves not only to take the TOEFL® iBT but also to perform well on the test.

We hope that everyone who uses *Decoding the TOEFL® iBT Actual Test Speaking 2* will be able to become more familiar with the TOEFL® iBT and will additionally improve his or her score on the test. As the title of the book implies, we hope that learners can use it to crack the code on the TOEFL® iBT, to make the test itself less mysterious and confusing, and to get the highest score possible. Finally, we hope that both learners and instructors can use this book to its full potential. We wish all of you the best of luck as you study English and prepare for the TOEFL® iBT, and we hope that *Decoding the TOEFL® iBT Actual Test Speaking 2* can provide you with assistance during the course of your studies.

Michael A. Putlack
Stephen Poirier
Tony Covello

TABLE
OF
CONTENTS

ABOUT THE TOEFL® iBT SPEAKING SECTION

How the Section Is Organized

The Speaking section is the third part of the TOEFL® iBT and consists of four questions. Question 1 is called the Independent Speaking Task and asks test takers to speak about a familiar topic. The other questions, questions 2-4, are called the Integrated Speaking Tasks. These tasks require test takers to integrate their speaking skills with other language skills such as listening and reading skills.

For each of the four questions, test takers are given preparation time and response time. During the preparation time, test takers can write down brief notes about how they will organize their responses. The preparation time ranges from 15 to 30 seconds, and the response time is either 45 or 60 seconds. The spoken responses are recorded and sent to be scored by raters. The raters evaluate responses based on three criteria: Delivery (how clear your speech is), Language Use (how effectively you use grammar and vocabulary to convey your ideas), and Topic Development (how fully you answer the question and how coherently you present your ideas).

Changes in the Speaking Section

The Speaking section is the section that has gone through the most drastic changes. Two question types – Questions 1 and 5 on the old test – have been removed. Therefore, the total number of questions has become four instead of six. Accordingly, the time allotted for the Speaking section has been reduced from 20 minutes to 17 minutes. However, the remaining questions have no changes, and the preparation times and the response times remain the same.

Question Types

TYPE 1 Independent Speaking Task: Question 1

The first question asks test takers to speak about a familiar topic. It is necessary for test takers to include specific examples and details in their response. After the question is presented, test takers are given 15 seconds to prepare their response and 45 seconds to speak.

Question 1 asks test takers to make a personal choice between two possible opinions, actions, or situations. In addition, on recent tests, test takers are sometimes given three options from which to choose, and they may be asked to speak about both the advantages and the disadvantages of a particular topic. Test takers are required to explain their choice by providing reasons and details. Topics for this question include everyday issues of general interest to test takers. For example, the question may ask about a preference between studying at home and studying at the library, a preference between living in a dormitory and living in an off-campus apartment, or a preference between a class with a lot of discussion and one without discussion.

ABOUT THE
TOEFL® iBT
SPEAKING SECTION

TYPE 2 **Integrated Speaking Tasks** (Reading, Listening, and Speaking): **Questions 2 and 3**

The second and third questions require test takers to integrate different language skills. Test takers are first presented with a short reading passage. The time given for reading is 45-50 seconds. After that, test takers will listen to a conversation or a lecture which is related to information presented in the reading passage. They need to organize their response by using information from both the reading passage and the conversation or lecture. For these questions, test takers are given 30 seconds to prepare their response and 60 seconds to speak.

Question 2 concerns a topic of campus-related interest, but it does not require prior firsthand experience of college or university life in North America to understand the topic. The reading passage is usually between 75 and 100 words long. It may be an announcement, letter, or article regarding a policy, rule, or future plan of a college or university. It can also be related to campus facilities or the quality of life on campus. After reading the passage, test takers will listen to two speakers discuss the topic presented in the reading passage. Typically, one of the two speakers shows a strong opinion about the topic. On recent tests, however, speakers have shown mixed feelings about the topic, so they like it yet also dislike some aspect of it. Test takers need to summarize the speaker's opinion and the reasons for holding it.

In Question 3, test takers will read a short passage about an academic subject and then listen to a professor lecture about that subject. The question requires test takers to relate the reading passage and the lecture. Topics for this question can be drawn from a variety of fields, including life science, social science, physical science, and the humanities. However, the question does not require prior knowledge of any particular field.

TYPE 3 **Integrated Speaking Tasks** (Listening and Speaking): **Question 4**

The last question presents only a listening passage—a lecture—and not a reading passage. Test takers need to respond based on what they hear. They are given 20 seconds to prepare their response and 60 seconds to speak.

For Question 4, test takers will listen to a lecture about an academic topic. As in Question 3, topics for this question can be drawn from a variety of fields, including life science, social science, physical science, and the humanities. Again, no prior knowledge is necessary to understand the lecture. After hearing the lecture, test takers are asked to summarize the lecture and to explain how the examples are connected with the overall topic.

Actual Test

01

CONTINUE

Speaking Section Directions

 Make sure your headset is on.

This section measures your ability to speak about a variety of topics. You will answer four questions by speaking into the microphone. Answer as completely as possible.

In the first question, you will speak about a familiar topic. Your response will be scored on your ability to speak clearly and coherently.

In the next two questions, you will first read a short reading passage. This passage will go away, and you will then listen to a talk on the same topic. You will be asked about the information you have read and heard. You will need to combine information from the reading passage and the talk to provide a complete answer. Your response will be scored on your ability to speak clearly and coherently and how accurately you convey information about what you read and heard.

In the last question, you will listen to part of a lecture. You will be asked about what you have heard. Your response will be scored on your ability to speak clearly and coherently and how accurately you convey information about what you heard.

You may take notes while you read and while you listen to the conversations and lectures. You may use your notes to help prepare your response.

Listen carefully to the directions for each question. The directions will not be written on the screen.

For each question, you will be given a short time to prepare your response (15 to 30 seconds, depending on the question). A clock will show how much preparation time is remaining. When the preparation time is up, you will be told to begin your response. A clock will show how much response time is remaining. A message will appear on the screen when the response time has ended.

AT01-01

Which of the following trips would you prefer to take?

• **A trip to one city during which you see many of the sights**

• **A trip to multiple cities during which you see a few sights in each place**

Use details and examples to explain your answer.

PREPARATION TIME
00:00:15

RESPONSE TIME
00:00:45

🎧 AT01-02

Special Weekly Event for Philosophy Majors

This semester, the Philosophy Department will hold a special weekly breakfast that all students majoring in Philosophy are invited to. The breakfast will be held each Wednesday from 7:30 to 8:30 and will be in the lounge on the first floor of Goddard Hall. All faculty in the department will be at the event. In addition, each breakfast will feature a guest speaker who will briefly discuss a topic of interest in the field of philosophy. For more information, contact Peter Welling at 535-6495. Reservations are required.

The woman expresses her opinion about the announcement by the Philosophy Department. Explain her opinion and the reasons she gives for holding that opinion.

PREPARATION TIME
00:00:30

RESPONSE TIME
00:00:60

AT01-03

Credence Purchases

Consumers know about the usefulness of many products they buy based on their previous experiences. However, in some cases, it is difficult to know how useful products will be before buying them, and it is sometimes hard to gauge their usefulness even after they have been purchased. Nevertheless, consumers still buy these products. These are credence purchases. Car repairs are an example of them. Most consumers have no idea whether the repairs mechanics make are helpful, yet, trusting the mechanics, they still pay for the repairs. And despite their ignorance, people frequently recommend the services of their mechanics to others.

The professor talks about his usage of vitamin supplements. Explain how his experience is related to credence purchases.

PREPARATION TIME
00:00:30

RESPONSE TIME
00:00:60

🎧 AT01-04

Using points and examples from the talk, explain how the bullsnake resembles the rattlesnake.

PREPARATION TIME
00:00:20

RESPONSE TIME
00:00:60

Actual Test

02

Speaking Section Directions

 Make sure your headset is on.

This section measures your ability to speak about a variety of topics. You will answer four questions by speaking into the microphone. Answer as completely as possible.

In the first question, you will speak about a familiar topic. Your response will be scored on your ability to speak clearly and coherently.

In the next two questions, you will first read a short reading passage. This passage will go away, and you will then listen to a talk on the same topic. You will be asked about the information you have read and heard. You will need to combine information from the reading passage and the talk to provide a complete answer. Your response will be scored on your ability to speak clearly and coherently and how accurately you convey information about what you read and heard.

In the last question, you will listen to part of a lecture. You will be asked about what you have heard. Your response will be scored on your ability to speak clearly and coherently and how accurately you convey information about what you heard.

You may take notes while you read and while you listen to the conversations and lectures. You may use your notes to help prepare your response.

Listen carefully to the directions for each question. The directions will not be written on the screen.

For each question, you will be given a short time to prepare your response (15 to 30 seconds, depending on the question). A clock will show how much preparation time is remaining. When the preparation time is up, you will be told to begin your response. A clock will show how much response time is remaining. A message will appear on the screen when the response time has ended.

AT02-01

Some people publicly share their thoughts on the Internet on blogs and social media. Others privately share their thoughts with their friends and family members. Which do you think is better and why? Use details and examples to explain your answer.

PREPARATION TIME
00:00:15

RESPONSE TIME
00:00:45

🎧 AT02-02

Book Checkout Regulation to Change

Starting immediately, students, staff, and faculty may only check out ten books from the university library system at one time. Previously, library users could borrow up to thirty books at once, but too many patrons have complained about large numbers of books being checked out from the libraries on campus and being continually renewed. Those individuals with more than ten books may keep the books they have but may not check out any new ones. Only after they have nine or fewer books checked out will they be permitted to borrow any new books.

The man expresses his opinion about the announcement by the library. Explain his opinion and the reasons he gives for holding that opinion.

PREPARATION TIME
00:00:30

RESPONSE TIME
00:00:60

AT02-03

Adaptive Reuse

When a building is no longer utilized for its original purpose, it is typically abandoned or destroyed. However, some people use their imaginations and find other usages for these buildings. In these cases, they are employing adaptive reuse. In recent years, adaptive reuse has become common in large cities. Old buildings, particularly those in sections originally designed for industry, are being converted from factories into apartment complexes, retail outlets, or other types of buildings. Adaptive reuse provides numerous benefits, including monetary savings and the reduction of urban sprawl since new buildings do not have to be constructed.

The professor talks about the plans for a new concert hall in the city. Explain how the new concert hall is related to adaptive reuse.

PREPARATION TIME
00:00:30

RESPONSE TIME
00:00:60

AT02-04

Using points and examples from the talk, explain two ways that marine life acquires nutrients.

PREPARATION TIME
00:00:20

RESPONSE TIME
00:00:60

Actual Test

03

Speaking Section Directions

 Make sure your headset is on.

This section measures your ability to speak about a variety of topics. You will answer four questions by speaking into the microphone. Answer as completely as possible.

In the first question, you will speak about a familiar topic. Your response will be scored on your ability to speak clearly and coherently.

In the next two questions, you will first read a short reading passage. This passage will go away, and you will then listen to a talk on the same topic. You will be asked about the information you have read and heard. You will need to combine information from the reading passage and the talk to provide a complete answer. Your response will be scored on your ability to speak clearly and coherently and how accurately you convey information about what you read and heard.

In the last question, you will listen to part of a lecture. You will be asked about what you have heard. Your response will be scored on your ability to speak clearly and coherently and how accurately you convey information about what you heard.

You may take notes while you read and while you listen to the conversations and lectures. You may use your notes to help prepare your response.

Listen carefully to the directions for each question. The directions will not be written on the screen.

For each question, you will be given a short time to prepare your response (15 to 30 seconds, depending on the question). A clock will show how much preparation time is remaining. When the preparation time is up, you will be told to begin your response. A clock will show how much response time is remaining. A message will appear on the screen when the response time has ended.

AT03-01

Do you agree or disagree with the following statement?

When students hand in their assignments late, teachers should lower their grades.

Use details and examples to explain your answer.

PREPARATION TIME
00:00:15

RESPONSE TIME
00:00:45

AT03-02

Writing Assignment for Theater Majors

All theater majors who are working on this semester's production of *Cat on a Hot Tin Roof* must submit a ten-page paper describing their experience with the play by November 27. Each paper should explain the student's role in the play and what the student learned. In return for doing this extra assignment, each student will be given three free tickets to the performance that may be sold for $15 apiece. And the students will be provided with free transportation between the school and the performing arts center downtown on the night of the play.

The man expresses his opinion about the announcement by the Theater Department. Explain his opinion and the reasons he gives for holding that opinion.

PREPARATION TIME
00:00:30

RESPONSE TIME
00:00:60

Tree Communication

Trees are able to communicate with one another in the form of chemicals they use to protect themselves when they are in danger. The scents of these chemicals are subsequently picked up by nearby trees, which then similarly protect themselves. For instance, when a tree is under attack by insects, it can release defensive chemicals that may either drive away the attackers or make itself less tasty to the insects. When the tree releases enough chemicals, they float on the air, and other trees detect them. They promptly react in the same manner to protect themselves as well.

The professor talks about how trees react when they are attacked by caterpillars. Explain how their actions are related to tree communication.

PREPARATION TIME
00:00:30

RESPONSE TIME
00:00:60

🎧 AT03-04

Using points and examples from the talk, explain two ways that people in ancient times used astronomy.

PREPARATION TIME
00:00:20

RESPONSE TIME
00:00:60

Actual Test

04

Speaking Section Directions

 Make sure your headset is on.

This section measures your ability to speak about a variety of topics. You will answer four questions by speaking into the microphone. Answer as completely as possible.

In the first question, you will speak about a familiar topic. Your response will be scored on your ability to speak clearly and coherently.

In the next two questions, you will first read a short reading passage. This passage will go away, and you will then listen to a talk on the same topic. You will be asked about the information you have read and heard. You will need to combine information from the reading passage and the talk to provide a complete answer. Your response will be scored on your ability to speak clearly and coherently and how accurately you convey information about what you read and heard.

In the last question, you will listen to part of a lecture. You will be asked about what you have heard. Your response will be scored on your ability to speak clearly and coherently and how accurately you convey information about what you heard.

You may take notes while you read and while you listen to the conversations and lectures. You may use your notes to help prepare your response.

Listen carefully to the directions for each question. The directions will not be written on the screen.

For each question, you will be given a short time to prepare your response (15 to 30 seconds, depending on the question). A clock will show how much preparation time is remaining. When the preparation time is up, you will be told to begin your response. A clock will show how much response time is remaining. A message will appear on the screen when the response time has ended.

🎧 AT04-01

Do you agree or disagree with the following statement?

It is easier to be a teacher than a student.

Use details and examples to explain your answer.

PREPARATION TIME
00:00:15

RESPONSE TIME
00:00:45

🎧 AT04-02

Fine Arts Majors to Do Student-Teaching

Starting this semester, all juniors and seniors in the Fine Arts Department must do student-teaching at a local elementary school or kindergarten. Each student must work at least once a week for two hours a day. There is a list of participating schools and kindergartens in the Fine Arts Department office in room 103 in Kilgore Hall. Students should consult the list and make their choices as soon as possible. Positions are available on a first-come, first-served basis. Call 303-6000 and ask to speak with Ron Donaldson for more details.

The woman expresses her opinion about the announcement by the Fine Arts Department. Explain her opinion and the reasons she gives for holding that opinion.

PREPARATION TIME

00:00:30

RESPONSE TIME

00:00:60

AT04-03

Resilient Ecosystems

Thriving ecosystems are those regions in which the organisms and natural elements are in balance with one another to the point that the ecosystems are not in any danger. However, if something disturbs the equilibrium, an ecosystem may suffer a significant upheaval. For example, if an ecosystem is exposed to a new source of pollution, it may be heavily damaged. Fortunately, most ecosystems have an inherent ability to overcome similar problems. These resilient ecosystems can therefore suffer disturbances but will eventually return to a state of equilibrium and once again thrive.

The professor talks about coral reef ecosystems. Explain how they are related to resilient ecosystems.

PREPARATION TIME
00:00:30

RESPONSE TIME
00:00:60

AT04-04

Using points and examples from the talk, explain two ways that tropical plants in high elevations have adapted to cold temperatures.

PREPARATION TIME

00:00:20

RESPONSE TIME

00:00:60

Actual Test

05

Speaking Section Directions

 Make sure your headset is on.

This section measures your ability to speak about a variety of topics. You will answer four questions by speaking into the microphone. Answer as completely as possible.

In the first question, you will speak about a familiar topic. Your response will be scored on your ability to speak clearly and coherently.

In the next two questions, you will first read a short reading passage. This passage will go away, and you will then listen to a talk on the same topic. You will be asked about the information you have read and heard. You will need to combine information from the reading passage and the talk to provide a complete answer. Your response will be scored on your ability to speak clearly and coherently and how accurately you convey information about what you read and heard.

In the last question, you will listen to part of a lecture. You will be asked about what you have heard. Your response will be scored on your ability to speak clearly and coherently and how accurately you convey information about what you heard.

You may take notes while you read and while you listen to the conversations and lectures. You may use your notes to help prepare your response.

Listen carefully to the directions for each question. The directions will not be written on the screen.

For each question, you will be given a short time to prepare your response (15 to 30 seconds, depending on the question). A clock will show how much preparation time is remaining. When the preparation time is up, you will be told to begin your response. A clock will show how much response time is remaining. A message will appear on the screen when the response time has ended.

VOLUME HELP NEXT

AT05-01

Do you agree or disagree with the following statement?

Playing computer or video games has a negative effect on teenagers.

Use details and examples to explain your answer.

PREPARATION TIME
00:00:15

RESPONSE TIME
00:00:45

AT05-02

Class Scheduling Problems

I strongly believe there is a problem with the way that classes are scheduled at this school. Currently, classes begin at the top of each hour and end ten minutes prior to the next hour. This leaves students with a mere ten minutes between classes. I think the break between classes should be extended to twenty minutes. Numerous times, I have wanted to discuss matters with my professors after class finished yet was not able to due to a lack of time. I hope the school seriously considers my suggestion and implements it next semester.

Carla Gant

Sophomore

The man expresses his opinion about the letter to the editor in the school newspaper. Explain his opinion and the reasons he gives for holding that opinion.

PREPARATION TIME
00:00:30

RESPONSE TIME
00:00:60

AT05-03

Logical Consequences

Logic is what allows people to realize that certain actions must follow when other actions occur. One element of logic involves the consequences of an action. If a person acts in a certain manner, logic dictates that there will be specific results. For instance, when a person is caught breaking the law, it is logical to assume that the individual will be punished. People are aware of these logical consequences because laws are passed to dissuade them from acting improperly. The punishment, however, must be severe enough that people will conclude that breaking the laws will result in serious consequences.

The professor talks about her experience as a teacher. Explain how it is related to logical consequences.

PREPARATION TIME
00:00:30

RESPONSE TIME
00:00:60

AT05-04

Using points and examples from the talk, explain how female rats changed when they became mothers.

PREPARATION TIME
00:00:20

RESPONSE TIME
00:00:60

Actual Test

06

Speaking Section Directions

 Make sure your headset is on.

This section measures your ability to speak about a variety of topics. You will answer four questions by speaking into the microphone. Answer as completely as possible.

In the first question, you will speak about a familiar topic. Your response will be scored on your ability to speak clearly and coherently.

In the next two questions, you will first read a short reading passage. This passage will go away, and you will then listen to a talk on the same topic. You will be asked about the information you have read and heard. You will need to combine information from the reading passage and the talk to provide a complete answer. Your response will be scored on your ability to speak clearly and coherently and how accurately you convey information about what you read and heard.

In the last question, you will listen to part of a lecture. You will be asked about what you have heard. Your response will be scored on your ability to speak clearly and coherently and how accurately you convey information about what you heard.

You may take notes while you read and while you listen to the conversations and lectures. You may use your notes to help prepare your response.

Listen carefully to the directions for each question. The directions will not be written on the screen.

For each question, you will be given a short time to prepare your response (15 to 30 seconds, depending on the question). A clock will show how much preparation time is remaining. When the preparation time is up, you will be told to begin your response. A clock will show how much response time is remaining. A message will appear on the screen when the response time has ended.

🎧 AT06-01

Do you agree or disagree with the following statement?

It is easier to teach students at elementary schools than students at universities.

Use details and examples to explain your answer.

PREPARATION TIME
00:00:15

RESPONSE TIME
00:00:45

AT06-02

Writing and Research Seminars to Be Held

During the first three weeks of the semester, the school is going to hold daily seminars that teach writing and research skills. All freshmen are strongly encouraged to sign up for and attend at least two of the seminars. These classes will be taught by a number of professors here on campus. Students will be able to apply the knowledge they learn in these seminars to the classes they are taking. Contact Shelby Morris in the office of the dean of students at 694-8312 for more information.

The woman expresses her opinion about the announcement by the dean of students. Explain her opinion and the reasons she gives for holding that opinion.

PREPARATION TIME
00:00:30

RESPONSE TIME
00:00:60

AT06-03

Close Communication Bias

People have close social systems consisting primarily of their family members and friends. Within these systems, communication between individuals sometimes breaks down. This happens because of the phenomenon called close communication bias. When people know others well, they may assume the individuals they are speaking with understand whatever it is they are discussing without requiring a detailed explanation. This typically results in a lack of understanding since important details are omitted. On the other hand, these people may explain the same thing in great detail to strangers since they lack familiarity with those people.

The professor talks about an incident involving two other professors and himself. Explain how that incident is related to close communication bias.

PREPARATION TIME
00:00:30

RESPONSE TIME
00:00:60

AT06-04

Using points and examples from the talk, explain how water striders are able to float and walk on water.

PREPARATION TIME

00:00:20

RESPONSE TIME

00:00:60

Actual Test

07

Speaking Section Directions

 Make sure your headset is on.

This section measures your ability to speak about a variety of topics. You will answer four questions by speaking into the microphone. Answer as completely as possible.

In the first question, you will speak about a familiar topic. Your response will be scored on your ability to speak clearly and coherently.

In the next two questions, you will first read a short reading passage. This passage will go away, and you will then listen to a talk on the same topic. You will be asked about the information you have read and heard. You will need to combine information from the reading passage and the talk to provide a complete answer. Your response will be scored on your ability to speak clearly and coherently and how accurately you convey information about what you read and heard.

In the last question, you will listen to part of a lecture. You will be asked about what you have heard. Your response will be scored on your ability to speak clearly and coherently and how accurately you convey information about what you heard.

You may take notes while you read and while you listen to the conversations and lectures. You may use your notes to help prepare your response.

Listen carefully to the directions for each question. The directions will not be written on the screen.

For each question, you will be given a short time to prepare your response (15 to 30 seconds, depending on the question). A clock will show how much preparation time is remaining. When the preparation time is up, you will be told to begin your response. A clock will show how much response time is remaining. A message will appear on the screen when the response time has ended.

🎧 AT07-01

Some people believe that a person needs to be talented to be a musician or painter. Others believe that training and hard work are more crucial. Which do you think is more important and why? Use details and examples to explain your answer.

PREPARATION TIME
00:00:15

RESPONSE TIME
00:00:45

🎧 AT07-02

Pete's Pizza to Close

Pete's Pizza, which has been located on the first floor of Wilson Hall for the past twelve years, is going to close its doors for the final time on October 12. Citing the increased costs of rent and salaries, the owner of Pete's Pizza, Pete Wellman, said he cannot make a profit on campus any more. "The school has doubled my rent in the past five years," he said. He added, "And I'm being pressured by the administration to pay my employees double the minimum wage. I can't do that, so the school won't rent to me any longer."

The man expresses his opinion about the article in the school newspaper. Explain his opinion and the reasons he gives for holding that opinion.

PREPARATION TIME
00:00:30

RESPONSE TIME
00:00:60

AT07-03

Animal Communication Problems

Animals communicate in a variety of manners, including using chemical, visual, and auditory means. It is not always easy for humans to understand what animals are communicating though. This is especially true if there is a slight variation in the method of signaling. A minute change may mean a great deal to animals when they communicate, but to human observers, the meaning may be lost. An additional problem is that humans frequently misinterpret what an animal's signal means based on their misunderstanding of a situation.

The professor talks about his dog. Explain how his dog's actions are related to animal communication problems.

PREPARATION TIME
00:00:30

RESPONSE TIME
00:00:60

🎧 AT07-04

Using points and examples from the talk, explain two ways that waders have adapted to find food in muddy areas.

PREPARATION TIME
00:00:20

RESPONSE TIME
00:00:60

Actual Test

08

Speaking Section Directions

 Make sure your headset is on.

This section measures your ability to speak about a variety of topics. You will answer four questions by speaking into the microphone. Answer as completely as possible.

In the first question, you will speak about a familiar topic. Your response will be scored on your ability to speak clearly and coherently.

In the next two questions, you will first read a short reading passage. This passage will go away, and you will then listen to a talk on the same topic. You will be asked about the information you have read and heard. You will need to combine information from the reading passage and the talk to provide a complete answer. Your response will be scored on your ability to speak clearly and coherently and how accurately you convey information about what you read and heard.

In the last question, you will listen to part of a lecture. You will be asked about what you have heard. Your response will be scored on your ability to speak clearly and coherently and how accurately you convey information about what you heard.

You may take notes while you read and while you listen to the conversations and lectures. You may use your notes to help prepare your response.

Listen carefully to the directions for each question. The directions will not be written on the screen.

For each question, you will be given a short time to prepare your response (15 to 30 seconds, depending on the question). A clock will show how much preparation time is remaining. When the preparation time is up, you will be told to begin your response. A clock will show how much response time is remaining. A message will appear on the screen when the response time has ended.

AT08-01

Do you agree or disagree with the following statement?

Everyone should be required to attend school until they are sixteen years old.

Use details and examples to explain your answer.

PREPARATION TIME
00:00:15

RESPONSE TIME
00:00:45

AT08-02

Remove TVs from Dorm Lounges

The school ought to get rid of the televisions that are located in all of the dormitory lounges. I have noticed that too many students spend hours watching various shows on TV. As a result, they are neglecting their studies. In addition, they are not communicating with their fellow students, so many students living on the same floor in a dormitory do not even know one another. Lastly, the noise from the TVs regularly disturbs students and prevents them from being able to study or sleep.

Alex Harper

Junior

The woman expresses her opinion about the letter to the editor in the school newspaper. Explain her opinion and the reasons she gives for holding that opinion.

PREPARATION TIME
00:00:30

RESPONSE TIME
00:00:60

AT08-03

Fake Signaling

In nature, organisms often utilize deception in order to survive. One type of deception, which is commonly used by predators to attract prey, is known as fake signaling. When using fake signaling, a predator sends out a signal that prey cannot resist and therefore follow back to its source. The prey is subsequently attacked by the predator. Fake signaling is typically used by predators that are able to secrete chemical signals which can mimic the female species of prey animals when they are ready to mate.

The professor talks about the female bolas spider. Explain how its actions are related to fake signaling.

PREPARATION TIME
00:00:30

RESPONSE TIME
00:00:60

🎧 AT08-04

Using points and examples from the talk, explain two benefits of flooding.

PREPARATION TIME
00:00:20

RESPONSE TIME
00:00:60

Actual Test

09

Speaking Section Directions

 Make sure your headset is on.

This section measures your ability to speak about a variety of topics. You will answer four questions by speaking into the microphone. Answer as completely as possible.

In the first question, you will speak about a familiar topic. Your response will be scored on your ability to speak clearly and coherently.

In the next two questions, you will first read a short reading passage. This passage will go away, and you will then listen to a talk on the same topic. You will be asked about the information you have read and heard. You will need to combine information from the reading passage and the talk to provide a complete answer. Your response will be scored on your ability to speak clearly and coherently and how accurately you convey information about what you read and heard.

In the last question, you will listen to part of a lecture. You will be asked about what you have heard. Your response will be scored on your ability to speak clearly and coherently and how accurately you convey information about what you heard.

You may take notes while you read and while you listen to the conversations and lectures. You may use your notes to help prepare your response.

Listen carefully to the directions for each question. The directions will not be written on the screen.

For each question, you will be given a short time to prepare your response (15 to 30 seconds, depending on the question). A clock will show how much preparation time is remaining. When the preparation time is up, you will be told to begin your response. A clock will show how much response time is remaining. A message will appear on the screen when the response time has ended.

AT09-01

Do you agree or disagree with the following statement?

Artists and musicians are not important to society.

Use details and examples to explain your answer.

PREPARATION TIME
00:00:15

RESPONSE TIME
00:00:45

AT09-02

Too Much Litter on Campus

I am a freshman in my first semester here, and I love this school. Unfortunately, I have noticed one enormous problem on campus: Too many students are littering. Instead of throwing their garbage away in trash cans, they are simply tossing it on the sidewalks or grass. I cannot believe how many times I have seen people carelessly littering on campus. I suggest that the school fine anyone who improperly disposes of trash $15. This should help decrease the number of people littering while simultaneously making the campus more beautiful.

Harold Barnes

Freshman

The woman expresses her opinion about the letter to the editor in the school newspaper. Explain her opinion and the reasons she gives for holding that opinion.

PREPARATION TIME
00:00:30

RESPONSE TIME
00:00:60

AT09-03

Teaser Advertising

One modern method of promoting products is to utilize teaser advertisement campaigns. A teaser advertisement is a short ad that prepares the public for a much larger ad campaign and the launch of a product in the future. Nowadays, this is a common way to promote films, television shows, and computer games. The advertisement may be just a few seconds long and may only provide a small glimpse of the product. It is used to tease the public and to build anticipation for its future unveiling.

The professor talks about movies. Explain how they are related to teaser advertising.

PREPARATION TIME
00:00:30

RESPONSE TIME
00:00:60

AT09-04

Using points and examples from the talk, explain how companies advertise based on the two types of demand.

PREPARATION TIME

00:00:20

RESPONSE TIME

00:00:60

Actual Test

10

Speaking Section Directions

 Make sure your headset is on.

This section measures your ability to speak about a variety of topics. You will answer four questions by speaking into the microphone. Answer as completely as possible.

In the first question, you will speak about a familiar topic. Your response will be scored on your ability to speak clearly and coherently.

In the next two questions, you will first read a short reading passage. This passage will go away, and you will then listen to a talk on the same topic. You will be asked about the information you have read and heard. You will need to combine information from the reading passage and the talk to provide a complete answer. Your response will be scored on your ability to speak clearly and coherently and how accurately you convey information about what you read and heard.

In the last question, you will listen to part of a lecture. You will be asked about what you have heard. Your response will be scored on your ability to speak clearly and coherently and how accurately you convey information about what you heard.

You may take notes while you read and while you listen to the conversations and lectures. You may use your notes to help prepare your response.

Listen carefully to the directions for each question. The directions will not be written on the screen.

For each question, you will be given a short time to prepare your response (15 to 30 seconds, depending on the question). A clock will show how much preparation time is remaining. When the preparation time is up, you will be told to begin your response. A clock will show how much response time is remaining. A message will appear on the screen when the response time has ended.

AT10-01

Which of the following do you prefer to do in class?

- **Take notes in a notebook while the teacher lectures**
- **Listen carefully to what the teacher says without taking any notes**

Use details and examples to explain your answer.

PREPARATION TIME
00:00:15

RESPONSE TIME
00:00:45

🎧 AT10-02

Best Student Academic Works to Be Published

All students are invited to submit one of their academic works for consideration to be published in an anthology at the end of the academic year. The school will publish the top fifteen academic papers in a hardcover book in May. All submissions must be made by March 1. Papers can be on any topic but must have been turned in for a class this school year. A group of ten professors will determine the winners, who will be announced on April 20. Papers may be turned in at the office of the dean of students in Warner Hall.

The man expresses his opinion about the announcement by the dean of students. Explain his opinion and the reasons he gives for holding that opinion.

PREPARATION TIME
00:00:30

RESPONSE TIME
00:00:60

AT10-03

Compromise Effect

When people are shopping, most of them do not want to buy the most expensive item available. Yet they do not desire to purchase the cheapest item either since it may not be of the best quality. In the end, most shoppers compromise by purchasing an item at a midrange price and hoping it is of good quality. Businesses are cognizant of the compromise effect and use this knowledge to their advantage. They frequently offer a higher-priced item, so shoppers eventually start purchasing the item which was once the most expensive one because they now regard it as reasonably priced.

The professor talks about how people make purchases of coffeemakers. Explain how their actions are related to the compromise effect.

PREPARATION TIME
00:00:30

RESPONSE TIME
00:00:60

🎧 AT10-04

Using points and examples from the talk, explain how people can survive extremely cold weather.

PREPARATION TIME
00:00:20

RESPONSE TIME
00:00:60

Actual Test

11

Speaking Section Directions

 Make sure your headset is on.

This section measures your ability to speak about a variety of topics. You will answer four questions by speaking into the microphone. Answer as completely as possible.

In the first question, you will speak about a familiar topic. Your response will be scored on your ability to speak clearly and coherently.

In the next two questions, you will first read a short reading passage. This passage will go away, and you will then listen to a talk on the same topic. You will be asked about the information you have read and heard. You will need to combine information from the reading passage and the talk to provide a complete answer. Your response will be scored on your ability to speak clearly and coherently and how accurately you convey information about what you read and heard.

In the last question, you will listen to part of a lecture. You will be asked about what you have heard. Your response will be scored on your ability to speak clearly and coherently and how accurately you convey information about what you heard.

You may take notes while you read and while you listen to the conversations and lectures. You may use your notes to help prepare your response.

Listen carefully to the directions for each question. The directions will not be written on the screen.

For each question, you will be given a short time to prepare your response (15 to 30 seconds, depending on the question). A clock will show how much preparation time is remaining. When the preparation time is up, you will be told to begin your response. A clock will show how much response time is remaining. A message will appear on the screen when the response time has ended.

AT11-01

Which would you prefer, to work in another city for more money or to work in the city you currently live in for less money? Use details and examples to explain your answer.

PREPARATION TIME
00:00:15

RESPONSE TIME
00:00:45

AT11-02

Students Banned from Selling Concessions at Events

Starting immediately, individual students and student organizations may no longer sell concessions at any school events. This includes football and basketball games, theatrical performances, and festivals such as homecoming. Too many students and student groups have been selling substandard or expired foods and beverages, which has caused some students to fall ill and others to be admitted to the hospital. The school is going to take over the selling of concessions at events. Any students seen trying to sell foods or drinks anywhere on campus will be reported to the university police.

The man expresses his opinion about the announcement by the school administration. Explain his opinion and the reasons he gives for holding that opinion.

PREPARATION TIME
00:00:30

RESPONSE TIME
00:00:60

AT11-03

Sound Masking

Some sounds are capable of masking or disrupting other ones. What happens is that one sound reduces a listener's ability to hear something else. Sound masking, as this is called, is often done intentionally to create a better sound environment by utilizing pleasing sounds to cover more unpleasant ones. However, this process can have negative results, too. For instance, the sound of an airplane taking off or landing can mask the one made by a television. And artificial noises made by humans are believed to have negative effects on animals that rely on sound to survive.

The professor talks about killer whales. Explain how their actions are related to sound masking.

PREPARATION TIME
00:00:30

RESPONSE TIME
00:00:60

AT11-04

Using points and examples from the talk, explain how predators and prey animals benefit by living in groups.

PREPARATION TIME
00:00:20

RESPONSE TIME
00:00:60

Actual Test

12

Speaking Section Directions

 Make sure your headset is on.

This section measures your ability to speak about a variety of topics. You will answer four questions by speaking into the microphone. Answer as completely as possible.

In the first question, you will speak about a familiar topic. Your response will be scored on your ability to speak clearly and coherently.

In the next two questions, you will first read a short reading passage. This passage will go away, and you will then listen to a talk on the same topic. You will be asked about the information you have read and heard. You will need to combine information from the reading passage and the talk to provide a complete answer. Your response will be scored on your ability to speak clearly and coherently and how accurately you convey information about what you read and heard.

In the last question, you will listen to part of a lecture. You will be asked about what you have heard. Your response will be scored on your ability to speak clearly and coherently and how accurately you convey information about what you heard.

You may take notes while you read and while you listen to the conversations and lectures. You may use your notes to help prepare your response.

Listen carefully to the directions for each question. The directions will not be written on the screen.

For each question, you will be given a short time to prepare your response (15 to 30 seconds, depending on the question). A clock will show how much preparation time is remaining. When the preparation time is up, you will be told to begin your response. A clock will show how much response time is remaining. A message will appear on the screen when the response time has ended.

AT12-01

Which do you prefer, seeing a movie or concert alone or in a group? Use details and examples to explain your answer.

PREPARATION TIME
00:00:15

RESPONSE TIME
00:00:45

AT12-02

Not Enough Electrical Outlets in Weston Hall

While the individual dormitory rooms in Weston Hall were nicely renovated during summer, one important problem was not corrected: There are not enough electrical outlets in the rooms. I live in a double in Weston Hall, and my room has two outlets, one of which can only take a single plug. My roommate and I both have computers, printers, and smartphones that need recharging. We also have a refrigerator and television. How are we supposed to use all of our appliances when multi-plug outlets are banned? The school needs to abolish the rule or add more outlets to each room.

Tina Weatherly

Senior

The woman expresses her opinion about the letter to the editor in the school newspaper. Explain her opinion and the reasons she gives for holding that opinion.

PREPARATION TIME
00:00:30

RESPONSE TIME
00:00:60

AT12-03

The Abilene Paradox

In 1974, a management expert wrote an article about what would eventually be called the Abilene Paradox because his example took place in Abilene, Texas. It refers to a time when all the members of a group have no interest in doing something. However, they erroneously believe the others want to do that activity, so they feel pressure to go along with them. Nobody wants to upset the group dynamics by voicing a negative opinion. Yet if one person in the group would express disinterest, the others would act similarly, and they could thereby avoid doing the activity nobody is interested in.

The professor talks about an incident involving his family. Explain how it is related to the Abilene Paradox.

PREPARATION TIME
00:00:30

RESPONSE TIME
00:00:60

AT12-04

Using points and examples from the talk, explain two situations in which animals may permit other animals of the same species to violate their territory.

PREPARATION TIME
00:00:20

RESPONSE TIME
00:00:60

Actual Test

13

Speaking Section Directions

 Make sure your headset is on.

This section measures your ability to speak about a variety of topics. You will answer four questions by speaking into the microphone. Answer as completely as possible.

In the first question, you will speak about a familiar topic. Your response will be scored on your ability to speak clearly and coherently.

In the next two questions, you will first read a short reading passage. This passage will go away, and you will then listen to a talk on the same topic. You will be asked about the information you have read and heard. You will need to combine information from the reading passage and the talk to provide a complete answer. Your response will be scored on your ability to speak clearly and coherently and how accurately you convey information about what you read and heard.

In the last question, you will listen to part of a lecture. You will be asked about what you have heard. Your response will be scored on your ability to speak clearly and coherently and how accurately you convey information about what you heard.

You may take notes while you read and while you listen to the conversations and lectures. You may use your notes to help prepare your response.

Listen carefully to the directions for each question. The directions will not be written on the screen.

For each question, you will be given a short time to prepare your response (15 to 30 seconds, depending on the question). A clock will show how much preparation time is remaining. When the preparation time is up, you will be told to begin your response. A clock will show how much response time is remaining. A message will appear on the screen when the response time has ended.

🎧 AT13-01

Do you agree or disagree with the following statement?

People in small towns are nicer than people in big cities.

Use details and examples to explain your answer.

PREPARATION TIME
00:00:15

RESPONSE TIME
00:00:45

AT13-02

Art Club to Be Established

There will be a new art club established this semester. All students, no matter what their major or GPA is, are invited to join the club. The only requirements are that the members enjoy art and attend the weekly meetings. This club will focus on art appreciation rather than its creation. So the members will frequently visit local museums and galleries. While these places charge entrance fees, all club members may gain admission at fifty percent off. Call 409-6495 and speak with Emily Burgess for more information.

The man expresses his opinion about the announcement by the student activities center. Explain his opinion and the reasons he gives for holding that opinion.

PREPARATION TIME
00:00:30

RESPONSE TIME
00:00:60

AT13-03

Oversimplification

When something is explained or described in terms so basic that its true meaning is lost, then oversimplification occurs. This commonly happens when people believe there is one simple explanation for a certain event. Yet most events are the result of complex interactions between various elements. Many people use oversimplification to allow for brevity when explaining something or to avoid going into detail because an issue is too complex for others to grasp easily. However, if an explanation is too rushed or is reduced to its most basic parts, misunderstandings will occur.

The professor talks about the American Revolution and World War II. Explain how they are related to oversimplification.

PREPARATION TIME
00:00:30

RESPONSE TIME
00:00:60

AT13-04

Using points and examples from the talk, explain two activities birds do before they migrate.

PREPARATION TIME
00:00:20

RESPONSE TIME
00:00:60

Actual Test

14

Speaking Section Directions

 Make sure your headset is on.

This section measures your ability to speak about a variety of topics. You will answer four questions by speaking into the microphone. Answer as completely as possible.

In the first question, you will speak about a familiar topic. Your response will be scored on your ability to speak clearly and coherently.

In the next two questions, you will first read a short reading passage. This passage will go away, and you will then listen to a talk on the same topic. You will be asked about the information you have read and heard. You will need to combine information from the reading passage and the talk to provide a complete answer. Your response will be scored on your ability to speak clearly and coherently and how accurately you convey information about what you read and heard.

In the last question, you will listen to part of a lecture. You will be asked about what you have heard. Your response will be scored on your ability to speak clearly and coherently and how accurately you convey information about what you heard.

You may take notes while you read and while you listen to the conversations and lectures. You may use your notes to help prepare your response.

Listen carefully to the directions for each question. The directions will not be written on the screen.

For each question, you will be given a short time to prepare your response (15 to 30 seconds, depending on the question). A clock will show how much preparation time is remaining. When the preparation time is up, you will be told to begin your response. A clock will show how much response time is remaining. A message will appear on the screen when the response time has ended.

🎧 AT14-01

Imagine that you are planning to sign up for a summer school class. Which of the following do you think would be the best class to sign up for?

- **A class you are interested in taking that has a strict professor**
- **A class that looks boring with a professor who gives high grades**
- **A class in your major with an average professor**

Use details and examples to explain your answer.

PREPARATION TIME
00:00:15

RESPONSE TIME
00:00:45

🎧 AT14-02

Graduation Speaker Named

City University is proud to announce that businessman Eric Carlyle is going to be the speaker at this spring's graduation ceremony, which will be held on May 14. Mr. Carlyle, who graduated from City University in 1984, is one of the country's foremost businessmen. He is a multibillionaire who has made fortunes in the automotive, computer, and robotics industries. His current interest is outer space, particularly establishing a colony on the moon and mining asteroids. Mr. Carlyle will be presented with an honorary doctorate at the graduation ceremony in honor of his numerous accomplishments.

The man expresses his opinion about the announcement by the school administration. Explain his opinion and the reasons he gives for holding that opinion.

PREPARATION TIME
00:00:30

RESPONSE TIME
00:00:60

AT14-03

Impression Management

A person's face often expresses the emotions he or she is feeling at the time. Thus it tends to be easy to tell, for instance, if a person is happy, angry, or sad. Yet sometimes it becomes necessary to manage one's facial expressions to avoid upsetting others. This is impression management. A situation is which this might be necessary is when someone is happy about another person's misfortune. A person who expresses joy at that time will likely make other individuals upset or uncomfortable. Thus the person needs to maintain a neutral or sympathetic expression to avoid causing problems.

The professor talks about an incident when she worked in an office. Explain how it is related to impression management.

PREPARATION TIME

00:00:30

RESPONSE TIME

00:00:60

AT14-04

Using points and examples from the talk, explain two ways in which the fourth wall may be treated by actors.

PREPARATION TIME

00:00:20

RESPONSE TIME

00:00:60

Actual Test

15

Speaking Section Directions

 Make sure your headset is on.

This section measures your ability to speak about a variety of topics. You will answer four questions by speaking into the microphone. Answer as completely as possible.

In the first question, you will speak about a familiar topic. Your response will be scored on your ability to speak clearly and coherently.

In the next two questions, you will first read a short reading passage. This passage will go away, and you will then listen to a talk on the same topic. You will be asked about the information you have read and heard. You will need to combine information from the reading passage and the talk to provide a complete answer. Your response will be scored on your ability to speak clearly and coherently and how accurately you convey information about what you read and heard.

In the last question, you will listen to part of a lecture. You will be asked about what you have heard. Your response will be scored on your ability to speak clearly and coherently and how accurately you convey information about what you heard.

You may take notes while you read and while you listen to the conversations and lectures. You may use your notes to help prepare your response.

Listen carefully to the directions for each question. The directions will not be written on the screen.

For each question, you will be given a short time to prepare your response (15 to 30 seconds, depending on the question). A clock will show how much preparation time is remaining. When the preparation time is up, you will be told to begin your response. A clock will show how much response time is remaining. A message will appear on the screen when the response time has ended.

AT15-01

Do you agree or disagree with the following statement?

The government should not spend money to protect endangered animals.

Use details and examples to explain your answer.

PREPARATION TIME
00:00:15

RESPONSE TIME
00:00:45

🎧 AT15-02

English 418 to Be Canceled

English 418 (Renaissance Poetry), which is taught by Professor Eva Bowman, has been canceled. Only seven students signed up for the class, and, according to school policy, there must be at least ten students enrolled for a class to be taught. Those wishing to study Renaissance poetry are encouraged to cross-enroll in English 78 (Poetry in the Renaissance), a class that is being taught at nearby Richardson College. To learn how to register for that class, please contact the English Department no later than this Friday, September 12.

The woman expresses her opinion about the announcement by the English Department. Explain her opinion and the reasons she gives for holding that opinion.

PREPARATION TIME
00:00:30

RESPONSE TIME
00:00:60

AT15-03

Defensive Pessimism

When people want to control their fears prior to an important event, they frequently use a strategy called defensive pessimism. These people think of all the negative things that could happen which might affect the outcome of the event. This type of thinking helps them plan for virtually every eventuality. While this may seem like a negative mental state, it actually helps individuals deal with their feelings of anxiety. By focusing on potential problems, people can channel their energy into solving them rather than on the fears they have.

The professor talks about his actions when he first started teaching. Explain how his actions are related to defensive pessimism.

PREPARATION TIME
00:00:30

RESPONSE TIME
00:00:60

AT15-04

Using points and examples from the talk, explain how fish overcome obstacles when they are migrating.

PREPARATION TIME
00:00:20

RESPONSE TIME
00:00:60

Actual Test

16

Speaking Section Directions

 Make sure your headset is on.

This section measures your ability to speak about a variety of topics. You will answer four questions by speaking into the microphone. Answer as completely as possible.

In the first question, you will speak about a familiar topic. Your response will be scored on your ability to speak clearly and coherently.

In the next two questions, you will first read a short reading passage. This passage will go away, and you will then listen to a talk on the same topic. You will be asked about the information you have read and heard. You will need to combine information from the reading passage and the talk to provide a complete answer. Your response will be scored on your ability to speak clearly and coherently and how accurately you convey information about what you read and heard.

In the last question, you will listen to part of a lecture. You will be asked about what you have heard. Your response will be scored on your ability to speak clearly and coherently and how accurately you convey information about what you heard.

You may take notes while you read and while you listen to the conversations and lectures. You may use your notes to help prepare your response.

Listen carefully to the directions for each question. The directions will not be written on the screen.

For each question, you will be given a short time to prepare your response (15 to 30 seconds, depending on the question). A clock will show how much preparation time is remaining. When the preparation time is up, you will be told to begin your response. A clock will show how much response time is remaining. A message will appear on the screen when the response time has ended.

AT16-01

Imagine that you are planning to visit an art gallery this weekend. Which of the following do you think would be the best way to see the artwork there?

- **You go alone and look at the paintings by yourself**

- **You go with a friend and discuss the artwork you see with your friend**

- **You go with a group of people who have different levels of interest in art**

Use details and examples to explain your answer.

PREPARATION TIME
00:00:15

RESPONSE TIME
00:00:45

AT16-02

Financial Aid Now Available

Beginning next semester, sophomores and juniors who wish to study abroad will be eligible to apply for financial assistance. Previously, students were required to pay all tuition, room and board, and other fees by themselves. However, sixty students a semester can now receive up to half the cost of tuition paid for in the form of a scholarship. Decisions on which students receive scholarships will be based upon both grades and financial need. Interested individuals should visit the study abroad office at 75 Timber Avenue or call 845-2643 for more information.

The woman expresses her opinion about the announcement by the university study abroad office. Explain her opinion and the reasons she gives for holding that opinion.

PREPARATION TIME
00:00:30

RESPONSE TIME
00:00:60

AT16-03

Tunnel Vision

Individuals with tunnel vision experience a loss of peripheral vision, which prevents them from seeing objects to either side of them. These objects are typically blurry or may not even be seen as the person is only capable of focusing on whatever is straight ahead. In psychology, people suffering from tunnel vision may be unable to consider alternative viewpoints and instead only accept their own opinions. Others may believe in stereotypes about people, particularly those individuals with certain characteristics or who belong to certain races.

The professor talks about his past experiences as a teacher and a policeman. Explain how they are related to tunnel vision.

PREPARATION TIME
00:00:30

RESPONSE TIME
00:00:60

AT16-04

Using points and examples from the talk, explain two ways that noise pollution affects people negatively.

PREPARATION TIME

00:00:20

RESPONSE TIME

00:00:60

Actual Test

17

Speaking Section Directions

 Make sure your headset is on.

This section measures your ability to speak about a variety of topics. You will answer four questions by speaking into the microphone. Answer as completely as possible.

In the first question, you will speak about a familiar topic. Your response will be scored on your ability to speak clearly and coherently.

In the next two questions, you will first read a short reading passage. This passage will go away, and you will then listen to a talk on the same topic. You will be asked about the information you have read and heard. You will need to combine information from the reading passage and the talk to provide a complete answer. Your response will be scored on your ability to speak clearly and coherently and how accurately you convey information about what you read and heard.

In the last question, you will listen to part of a lecture. You will be asked about what you have heard. Your response will be scored on your ability to speak clearly and coherently and how accurately you convey information about what you heard.

You may take notes while you read and while you listen to the conversations and lectures. You may use your notes to help prepare your response.

Listen carefully to the directions for each question. The directions will not be written on the screen.

For each question, you will be given a short time to prepare your response (15 to 30 seconds, depending on the question). A clock will show how much preparation time is remaining. When the preparation time is up, you will be told to begin your response. A clock will show how much response time is remaining. A message will appear on the screen when the response time has ended.

AT17-01

Answer one of the following questions.

1   Some students prefer to learn by watching videos while others prefer to learn by taking classes with teachers. Talk about the advantages and disadvantages of learning by watching videos. Use details and examples to explain your answer.

2   Some students prefer to learn by watching videos while others prefer to learn by taking classes with teachers. Talk about the advantages and disadvantages of learning by taking classes with teachers. Use details and examples to explain your answer.

PREPARATION TIME
00:00:15

RESPONSE TIME
00:00:45

🎧 AT17-02

New Policy on Reference Books

Students, faculty, and staff members may now check out books from the reference section of Harper Library. They are only permitted to check these books out for two days though. Regular books may still be borrowed for a period of two weeks and may be renewed up to three times. Reference books are not allowed to be renewed. In addition, any patron who damages or loses a reference book will be charged either a repair fee or a lost book fee, respectively, that reflects the high costs of most reference materials.

The man expresses his opinion about the notice by the university library. Explain his opinion and the reasons he gives for holding that opinion.

PREPARATION TIME
00:00:30

RESPONSE TIME
00:00:60

🎧 AT17-03

Relationship Marketing

In recent years, some marketing efforts have moved beyond simply focusing on making sales of goods and services to customers. Instead, marketing campaigns today often focus on retaining customers and developing long-term relationships with them. Businesses may do this by providing outstanding services or products for their customers. They might also provide customers with various perks that encourage customers to have extensive and continuous dealings with those companies. By using relationship marketing, businesses try to obtain maximum value from their customers over a long period of time.

The professor talks about a trip he took in the past. Explain how it is related to relationship marketing.

PREPARATION TIME
00:00:30

RESPONSE TIME
00:00:60

AT17-04

Using points and examples from the talk, explain how the ancient Egyptians and Mesopotamians irrigated their fields.

PREPARATION TIME
00:00:20

RESPONSE TIME
00:00:60

Actual Test

18

Speaking Section Directions

 Make sure your headset is on.

This section measures your ability to speak about a variety of topics. You will answer four questions by speaking into the microphone. Answer as completely as possible.

In the first question, you will speak about a familiar topic. Your response will be scored on your ability to speak clearly and coherently.

In the next two questions, you will first read a short reading passage. This passage will go away, and you will then listen to a talk on the same topic. You will be asked about the information you have read and heard. You will need to combine information from the reading passage and the talk to provide a complete answer. Your response will be scored on your ability to speak clearly and coherently and how accurately you convey information about what you read and heard.

In the last question, you will listen to part of a lecture. You will be asked about what you have heard. Your response will be scored on your ability to speak clearly and coherently and how accurately you convey information about what you heard.

You may take notes while you read and while you listen to the conversations and lectures. You may use your notes to help prepare your response.

Listen carefully to the directions for each question. The directions will not be written on the screen.

For each question, you will be given a short time to prepare your response (15 to 30 seconds, depending on the question). A clock will show how much preparation time is remaining. When the preparation time is up, you will be told to begin your response. A clock will show how much response time is remaining. A message will appear on the screen when the response time has ended.

AT18-01

Which of the following should parents do regarding the television programs their children view?

• **Allow them to watch any programs they are interested in**

• **Monitor their viewing and only allow them to watch preapproved programs**

Use details and examples to explain your answer.

PREPARATION TIME
00:00:15

RESPONSE TIME
00:00:45

AT18-02

Minter Dining Hall Open to Everyone

As of October 1, Minter Dining Hall will be open to everyone on campus. Minter has long been the sole faculty dining facility on campus, and students and university employees were previously only permitted to dine in it if they were accompanied by a professor. Due to lobbying by both the student body and members of the school administration, the dining hall's rules are being changed. The prices of breakfast, lunch, and dinner at Minter Dining Hall will remain fifty percent higher than those at other dining facilities though.

The man expresses his opinion about the announcement by the student dining services office. Explain his opinion and the reasons he gives for holding that opinion.

PREPARATION TIME
00:00:30

RESPONSE TIME
00:00:60

AT18-03

Free-Rider Effect

There are often resources and various goods and services which are provided by one person, business, or government but which are used by others. When the others using them fail to pay for their use—or only pay a small amount—then they are considered free riders. Essentially, these people are benefiting from the actions of others while contributing little or nothing themselves. Over time, the free-rider effect can lead to problems concerning the providing of various goods and services due to a lack of financing.

The professor talks about the local roads and a local museum. Explain how they are related to the free-rider effect.

PREPARATION TIME
00:00:30

RESPONSE TIME
00:00:60

AT18-04

Using points and examples from the talk, explain two types of linear parks found in urban centers these days.

PREPARATION TIME

00:00:20

RESPONSE TIME

00:00:60

Actual Test

19

Speaking Section Directions

 Make sure your headset is on.

This section measures your ability to speak about a variety of topics. You will answer four questions by speaking into the microphone. Answer as completely as possible.

In the first question, you will speak about a familiar topic. Your response will be scored on your ability to speak clearly and coherently.

In the next two questions, you will first read a short reading passage. This passage will go away, and you will then listen to a talk on the same topic. You will be asked about the information you have read and heard. You will need to combine information from the reading passage and the talk to provide a complete answer. Your response will be scored on your ability to speak clearly and coherently and how accurately you convey information about what you read and heard.

In the last question, you will listen to part of a lecture. You will be asked about what you have heard. Your response will be scored on your ability to speak clearly and coherently and how accurately you convey information about what you heard.

You may take notes while you read and while you listen to the conversations and lectures. You may use your notes to help prepare your response.

Listen carefully to the directions for each question. The directions will not be written on the screen.

For each question, you will be given a short time to prepare your response (15 to 30 seconds, depending on the question). A clock will show how much preparation time is remaining. When the preparation time is up, you will be told to begin your response. A clock will show how much response time is remaining. A message will appear on the screen when the response time has ended.

AT19-01

Which of the following universities would you prefer to attend?

- **A school that has excellent professors and facilities but high tuition**

- **A school with average professors and facilities but is free to attend**

Use details and examples to explain your answer.

PREPARATION TIME
00:00:15

RESPONSE TIME
00:00:45

AT19-02

New Dormitory Policy

After careful consideration, the university administration has decided to permit juniors and seniors living on campus to stay in dormitory rooms by themselves. 250 rooms in Walker Hall, Stuart Hall, and Grant Hall will be converted into single rooms during the summer. Those individuals wishing to live in single rooms should sign up at the student housing office. A lottery will be held to determine which students can stay in the rooms. The price of a single room will be approximately twice that of staying in a double room.

The woman expresses her opinion about the notice by the university student housing office. Explain her opinion and the reasons she gives for holding that opinion.

PREPARATION TIME
00:00:30

RESPONSE TIME
00:00:60

AT19-03

Upward Comparison

People often make comparisons between themselves and others, especially those individuals whom they believe are better off than they are in some way. In many instances, people make comparisons in order to determine how to improve their lives, and then they make positive changes. There are also negative effects of upward comparison though. People may experience feelings of envy or jealousy upon seeing how others are doing better or are more successful than they are. How the people making the upward comparisons react to these feeling differs but is often negative.

The professor talks about two of his friends from college. Explain how their actions are related to upward comparison.

PREPARATION TIME
00:00:30

RESPONSE TIME
00:00:60

🎧 AT19-04

Using points and examples from the talk, explain how Pampas grass and the ombu thrive in the Pampas grasslands.

PREPARATION TIME
00:00:20

RESPONSE TIME
00:00:60

Actual Test

20

Speaking Section Directions

 Make sure your headset is on.

This section measures your ability to speak about a variety of topics. You will answer four questions by speaking into the microphone. Answer as completely as possible.

In the first question, you will speak about a familiar topic. Your response will be scored on your ability to speak clearly and coherently.

In the next two questions, you will first read a short reading passage. This passage will go away, and you will then listen to a talk on the same topic. You will be asked about the information you have read and heard. You will need to combine information from the reading passage and the talk to provide a complete answer. Your response will be scored on your ability to speak clearly and coherently and how accurately you convey information about what you read and heard.

In the last question, you will listen to part of a lecture. You will be asked about what you have heard. Your response will be scored on your ability to speak clearly and coherently and how accurately you convey information about what you heard.

You may take notes while you read and while you listen to the conversations and lectures. You may use your notes to help prepare your response.

Listen carefully to the directions for each question. The directions will not be written on the screen.

For each question, you will be given a short time to prepare your response (15 to 30 seconds, depending on the question). A clock will show how much preparation time is remaining. When the preparation time is up, you will be told to begin your response. A clock will show how much response time is remaining. A message will appear on the screen when the response time has ended.

AT20-01

An area of historical interest is discovered in your local area. Which of the following groups of people should the city permit to visit it?

- **All members of the public who are willing to pay an admission fee**

- **Only experts who work to help preserve the site**

- **Only people who have college degrees in either history or archaeology**

Use details and examples to explain your answer.

PREPARATION TIME
00:00:15

RESPONSE TIME
00:00:45

AT20-02

University to Develop New Land

More than fifty acres of land between Eastern Road and the Trident River were recently acquired by the university. This land, which is currently unoccupied, will be developed over the course of the next year. Once the first stage of the development process is complete, several new buildings will be constructed. They will be the location of the new law school that the university intends to open three years from now. Plans for the development process may be viewed at the development office in 309 West Hall.

The man expresses his opinion about the announcement by the university development office. Explain his opinion and the reasons he gives for holding that opinion.

PREPARATION TIME
00:00:30

RESPONSE TIME
00:00:60

🎧 AT20-03

Artificial Environments

Artificial environments are attempts by humans to create ecosystems which do not appear or form in the real world under natural conditions. They are typically characterized by a lack of diversity with regard to both plant and animal life. The food chain is therefore almost always irrelevant in them. They are also not sustainable without human intervention in some manner. Unless humans act, artificial environments would quickly either fall apart or revert to the state in which they existed naturally without any prior interference from humans.

The professor talks about greenhouses and farms. Explain how they are related to artificial environments.

PREPARATION TIME
00:00:30

RESPONSE TIME
00:00:60

🎧 AT20-04

Using points and examples from the talk, explain two limitations of solar power in urban centers.

PREPARATION TIME
00:00:20

RESPONSE TIME
00:00:60

Memo

AUTHORS

Michael A. Putlack
- MA in History, Tufts University, Medford, MA, USA
- Expert test developer of TOEFL, TOEIC, and TEPS
- Main author of the Darakwon *How to Master Skills for the TOEFL® iBT* series and *TOEFL® MAP* series

Stephen Poirier
- Candidate for PhD in History, University of Western Ontario, Canada
- Certificate of Professional Technical Writing, Carleton University, Canada
- Co-author of the Darakwon *How to Master Skills for the TOEFL® iBT* series and *TOEFL® MAP* series

Tony Covello
- BA in Political Science, Beloit College, Beloit, WI, USA
- MA in TEFL, International Graduate School of English, Seoul, Korea
- Term instructor at George Mason University Korea, Songdo, Incheon, Korea

Decoding the **TOEFL**® iBT
Actual Test **SPEAKING** 2 NEW TOEFL® EDITION

Publisher Chung Kyudo
Editors Kim Minju
Authors Michael A. Putlack, Stephen Poirier, Tony Covello
Proofreader Michael A. Putlack
Designers Koo Soojung, Park Sunyoung

First published in March 2020
By Darakwon, Inc.
Darakwon Bldg., 211, Munbal-ro, Paju-si, Gyeonggi-do 10881
Republic of Korea
Tel: 82-2-736-2031 (Ext. 250)
Fax: 82-2-732-2037

ISBN 978-89-277-0869-8 14740
          978-89-277-0862-9 14740 (set)

www.darakwon.co.kr

Components Test Book / Answer Book
8 7 6 5 4 3 2   23 24 25 26 27

Decoding the TOEFL® iBT

Actual Test

SPEAKING 2 Scripts &
Sample Answers

Actual Test 01

Question 1 p. 9

Sample Answer 1

Trip to One City

1 **can see many sights**
   - went to Paris for five days
   - explored many places → trip was worthwhile

2 **vacation should be restful**
   - if go to many cities, spend lots of time traveling
   - would make me tired

Sample Response

I understand why some people would prefer to travel to multiple cities, but I think it's much better to visit only one city when you go on vacation. To begin with, by visiting a single city, you can see as many of the sights there as possible. For instance, my family took a five-day trip to Paris, France, last year. Instead of just visiting the Louvre Museum and the Eiffel Tower, we got to explore many places in Paris, and that made the trip worthwhile. Another thing is that when you go on vacation, it should be restful. If you travel to multiple cities, you have to spend lots of time either on buses or airplanes going from place to place. Doing that would make me too tired.

Sample Answer 2

Trip to Multiple Cities

1 **don't travel much → want to visit many places**
   - tours of Europe = 6 countries in one week
   - ideal for me

2 **don't need to know city in depth**
   - want to see highlights of city
   - stay 1-2 days and then go to next place

Sample Response

Of the two choices, I would be in favor of visiting multiple cities. First, I don't often get to go on trips, so when the opportunity arises, I'd love to travel to as many places as possible. I have heard about some tours of Europe in which people visit around six countries in a week. For me, that would be an ideal trip because I'd get to tour so many places. Second, I'm not particularly interested in getting to know a city in depth. Instead, I'd prefer to see the highlights and most attractive places in a city. In most cases, that involves only being there for one or two days. After I see the best spots, I'm ready to move on and to check out another place.

Question 2 p. 10

Listening Script

Now listen to two students discussing the announcement.

M Student: Who were you talking to on the phone just now?

W Student: I called Peter Welling in the Philosophy Department to make a reservation for the upcoming special breakfast.

M: You're actually going to attend it? It seems like it will be pretty boring to me.

W: Well, I found out from Mr. Welling that the guest speaker is going to be Dr. Richard Thomas, who's a very big name in the field. I read his most recent book and loved it. Oh, and Mr. Welling said there will be other similar speakers this semester, so it will be a good chance to learn while having breakfast.

M: Hmm . . . I suppose you could be right.

W: You should make a reservation and go along with me. It will be fun, and there's one more advantage to going.

M: What's that?

W: Free breakfast, of course. It will be nice not to have to eat the same food we get for breakfast at the dining hall every day. I get tired of dining hall food really quickly.

Sample Answer

Reading Note

Special breakfast for Philosophy majors

- faculty will be there
- each breakfast → has guest speaker

Listening Note

Woman → supports breakfast

1 **wants to hear guest speaker**
   - knows first speaker → read book
   - will be other similar speakers later

2 **wants free breakfast**
   - will be different from dining hall food
   - gets tired of that food

Sample Response

According to the announcement by the Philosophy Department, there is going to be a special breakfast held each Wednesday during the semester. Philosophy majors are invited to attend it with the faculty, and there will be a guest speaker at each breakfast. The woman tells the man that she likes the news in the announcement for a couple of reasons. First, she says that she is familiar with the work of the first guest speaker and notes that she even read his book. She states that the guest speaker each week will be a notable person, so she hopes to learn at the events. The woman also points out that the breakfast they will be served will be different than the breakfast at the dining hall. She comments that she gets tired of eating the same breakfast every day, so it will be nice to have something different for a change.

Question 3

p. 11

Listening Script

Now listen to a lecture on this topic in an economics class.

M Professor: You all know what credence purchases are, right? Well, uh, let me give you an example of one just in case you're not completely clear on the concept. Now, uh, like lots of people, I buy and use vitamin supplements despite the fact that I'm not quite sure if they're good for me. Sure, uh, experts say they're helpful, and so do the commercials on TV, but we can't really tell, can we?

A couple of months ago, I saw an ad for calcium supplements, which are supposed to make your bones stronger. I'm in my fifties, so I thought I ought to take them. I bought the supplements and have been taking them, but I have no idea how effective they are. After all, can I feel my bones getting stronger . . . ? No, I can't.

But the funny thing is that after I started taking them, I recommended the calcium supplements to my friends in spite of my lack of proof. Why did I do that . . . ? Well, I had spent good money on them, so I felt they must have been effective. And to justify my spending, I told people who asked me that the supplements were a good product. I did that even though I had no actual evidence that they were working as they were supposed to.

Sample Answer

Reading Note

Credence Purchases

don't know usefulness of product yet still buy

- car repairs = credence purchase
- don't know if repairs are helpful but pay for them → may recommend to others

Listening Note

bought calcium supplements

- getting older → wants strong bones
- doesn't know how effective they are

recommended them to friends

- had spent $ on them → must have been effective
- justified buying them → said was good product

Sample Response

The professor tells the students about his recent experience with calcium supplements. He says that since he is getting older, he decided to take some supplements because they're supposed to be good for his bones. After taking the supplements, he wasn't sure if they were helping his body or not. Even though he didn't know if they were good for him, he told his friends about the supplements and encouraged them to buy them. He says he did that because he wanted to justify the money that he spent on the supplements. The professor's actions are an example of a credence purchase. This is a purchase that a person makes out of trust. The reason is that the individual has no idea about the effectiveness of the product that he or she purchases, but the person merely has faith that the money was well spent.

Question 4

p. 12

Listening Script

Listen to part of a lecture in a zoology class.

M Professor: Unlike most people, I happen to have a soft spot for snakes. One of the snakes I like the most is the bullsnake. It's a nonvenomous snake found primarily in Western Canada and the Great Plains region of the United States. Here's a picture of it . . . It averages a bit less than two meters in length . . . Notice the yellowish-brown color of its skin as well as the pattern on it. It looks like a rattlesnake, which is a highly venomous snake, doesn't it . . . ? This form of mimicry provides a number of benefits for the bullsnake. Let me explain . . .

The bullsnake actually mimics the rattlesnake in ways extending beyond its skin. It's capable of making a sound similar to the rattlesnake's warning rattle. It does this by forcing air through its mouth to produce a hissing sound. The sound created is so similar to a rattlesnake's rattle that people and animals frequently mistake the sound as coming from the more dangerous rattlesnake. A bullsnake can also rapidly move its tail in dry grass to simulate a rattling sound. In that way, it can ward off predators by mimicking the actions of the venomous rattlesnake.

A second act of mimicry happens when the bullsnake shapes its body to resemble the body of the rattlesnake. The bullsnake can make a curved S-shape like a rattlesnake that's about to strike. It can flatten and puff out its round head so that it's more like the diamond-shaped head of the rattlesnake as well. The bullsnake is so good at imitating the rattlesnake that people sometimes kill it to protect themselves. While the bullsnake will bite if it's cornered, it has no venom. So, uh, the bite would be painful but not fatal.

Listening Note

Bullsnake = uses mimicry to look like rattlesnake

1 **makes sound like rattlesnake's warning rattle**
   - makes hissing sound w/mouth
   - moves tail in dry grass → sounds like rattle

2 **shapes body to resemble rattlesnake**
   - makes curved S-shape of rattlesnake
   - flattens and puffs out round head →
     looks like diamond-shaped head of rattlesnake

Sample Response

The professor shows a picture of a bullsnake to the class and points out how it resembles the rattlesnake. He says that the skin color and patterns on the skin make the bullsnake look like the rattlesnake. Then, he describes two types of behavior that enable the bullsnake to mimic the rattlesnake. Firstly, the bullsnake can imitate the rattlesnake's warning rattle by producing a hissing sound from its mouth. It also sometimes moves its tail in grass to create a rattling sound. These two actions can scare off predators since they don't want to attack a snake they believe is venomous. Secondly, the bullsnake can change the way its head looks. It can flatten its head to make an S-shape that resembles the head of a rattlesnake ready to strike. When the bullsnake does that, it confuses both people and animals and makes them believe it is a rattlesnake in reality.

Actual Test 02

Question 1 p. 15

Sample Answer 1

Share Thoughts Publicly

1 **shouldn't be afraid to say real thoughts**
   - write thoughts on my blog
   - not scared to let people know my beliefs

2 **can meet others if honest about thoughts**
   - others think the same way
   - can easily meet if write thoughts online

Sample Response

I'm the kind of person who believes people should be proud of their beliefs no matter what they are, so I think it would be better for people to share their thoughts on the Internet on blogs and social media. First of all, many people are afraid to say what they really think about someone or something. Personally, I think people shouldn't be that way. I have my own blog, and I write whatever I want on it. My beliefs are my beliefs, and I'm not scared to let people know what they are. Second of all, if people were more honest about their thoughts, they'd be able to meet other individuals who feel the same way. By broadcasting their beliefs online, they'd be able easily to accomplish that goal.

Sample Answer 2

Share Thoughts Privately

1 **people may disagree w/you**
   - may leave bad comments
   - may contact school or workplace and cause problems

2 **am private person**
   - only want to speak w/friends and family
   - don't want others involved in my life

Sample Response

Nowadays, sharing your thoughts online can be incredibly risky, so I'm in favor of only sharing my thoughts with my friends and family members. One reason is that if you make a controversial announcement on the Internet, some people who disagree with you may leave nasty comments on your blog or homepage. Others might even contact your school or employer and try to get you suspended or fired. Another reason is that I'm a fairly private person, so I'm only interested in speaking with my friends and family members. I couldn't care less what other people think about me, so I see no reason to announce my beliefs online and to encourage people that I don't know to involve themselves in my life.

Question 2 p. 16

Listening Script

Now listen to two students discussing the announcement.

W Student: Keith, you're always in the library. What do you think of the new policy being enacted?

M Student: I fully support it.

W: No kidding? I'm surprised. I figured you'd be against it because you have so many books checked out.

M: On the contrary, I check out few books despite spending several hours a day in the library.

W: So, uh, what makes you support the new rule?

M: First of all, it will allow more students to borrow books. It's really frustrating to look up a book you need on the library's computer system only to find out it has already been checked out. Thanks to this new rule, there will be more books on the shelves.

W: Okay, but if people can't check the books out, how will they be able to use them?

M: Easy. They can photocopy the relevant pages. I have a friend who works in the library, and she told me the library is going to install more photocopiers and lower the price of making copies.

W: Wow, that's cool.

M: Exactly. Since making copies will be cheaper, more students will do that rather than check out books, so more books can remain in the library.

Sample Answer

Reading Note

Can only check out 10 books at time

- many books checked out from library
- need to return if have more than 10 checked out

Listening Note

Man → supports the regulation

1 **will let students check out more books**
   - need book but is checked out = frustrating
   - will be more books on shelves

2 **can photocopy needed pages**
   - library will buy more copiers + lower price of copies
   - students can make copies so books stay in library

Sample Response

The man tells the woman that he supports the announcement by the library. The library is changing its rules so that people can no longer check out up to thirty books at a time. Instead, they can only borrow ten books. The library is enacting the change because too many of its users are complaining about large numbers of books being checked out. The man tells the woman that this is a good decision for a couple of reasons. He points out how annoying it is to need a book at the library but then to find out that someone else has already borrowed it. Then, he tells the woman that he knows the library is going to add more copy machines and decrease the price of making copies. This will be done to encourage students to photocopy pages from books rather than to check them out.

Question 3

p. 17

Listening Script

Now listen to a lecture on this topic in an architecture class.

W Professor: Today, I'd like to show you the architectural plans of a building that's going to be refurbished in our city's old industrial park, and this will illustrate the concept of adaptive reuse. Take a look at the screen . . . You can see a picture of the old Clemens Chocolate Factory on First Avenue. The city bought the building a year ago and intends to transform it into a concert hall.

Now, look up here . . . These are the architectural plans for the concert hall. Notice that one half of the factory's second floor has been removed . . . while the other half of the second floor will be a balcony section. Here on the, um, main floor will be the stage . . . the orchestra pit . . . and the main seating area.

Aside from this . . . oh, and the upgrades in electrical wiring and plumbing, of course . . . little else will be changed in the building. For instance, its original shell will remain intact. The high glass windows, which provide plenty of light, will remain, and so will the ceiling. The city estimates it will save up to ten million dollars by transforming the factory into a concert hall instead of erecting an entirely new building. And it can put the concert hall downtown rather than constructing it somewhere on the outskirts of the city.

Sample Answer

Reading Note

Adaptive Reuse

find other uses for buildings

- common in large cities
- convert factories into apartments, stores, and others
- can save $ and reduce urban sprawl

Listening Note

will refurbish building in old industrial park

- turn into concert hall
- make some changes to

will save $ for city

- save up to $10 million
- don't have to erect new building
- can put building downtown, not in outskirts

Sample Response

The professor lectures to the students about a concert hall the city is planning to make. It purchased an old factory and is going to renovate it to transform it into a concert hall. The professor shows the plans for the building to the students and points out how parts of it need to be changed. But she also stresses that many parts of the building, including its original shell, windows, and ceilings, are not going to be changed. She declares that the city will save millions of dollars by using an existing building rather than making a new one. And she adds that the concert hall can therefore be built downtown instead of somewhere else. The city's plans for the concert hall are an example of adaptive reuse. This involves the reusing of a building for a reason other than its usual purpose. This can save money and reduce urban sprawl.

Question 4

p. 18

Listening Script

Listen to part of a lecture in a marine biology class.

M Professor: Now, um, let me talk for a bit about how marine life forms acquire the nutrients they need to survive. Most marine life, especially fish, does this simply by chasing down prey, catching it, and eating it. Yet this isn't easy for all forms of life in the ocean, particularly those which are either, um, very slow or mostly inactive. These creatures have to, well, they have to come up with other more specialized ways to acquire food. Some methods are active while others are passive.

The sea anemone is a creature that's somewhat inactive yet utilizes active measures to get the nutrients it requires. Here's a picture of it . . . Notice that it's a flowerlike animal. In fact, it's a polyp, so it attaches itself to the seafloor. Fish are attracted to it, and, uh, as they swim by, the sea anemone's tentacles reach out, touch the fish, and release venom. The venom paralyzes the fish, thereby allowing the sea anemone to draw the fish toward its mouth, which is in the center of its body. In this way, the sea anemone employs a fairly active measure to feed itself.

The oyster, on the other hand . . . here's a picture . . . has a very passive feeding method. Like the sea anemone, it lies on the seafloor, yet it lacks the ability to prey on other creatures. So it merely passes water through its shell. It has many tiny hairs, called ctenidia. That's spelled C-T-E-N-I-D-I-A. These hairs filter out nutrients, such as plankton, and move them toward the oyster's mouth. Because of this passive way of feeding itself, oysters are known as filter feeders.

Sample Answer

Listening Note

Some sea creatures = specialized ways to acquire food

1 **sea anemone = inactive yet uses active measures to get food**
   - flowerlike animal → fish attracted to → grabs fish w/tentacles
   - tentacles release venom → paralyze fish → can eat

2 **oyster = has passive feeding method**
   - lets water pass through shell
   - ctenidia → hairs that filter nutrients such as plankton

Sample Response

During his lecture, the professor tells the students there are some animals that live in the sea which can't hunt prey like most other animals do. He points out that these forms of marine life may use either active or passive ways to get nutrients. The sea anemone utilizes active measures to get food. The professor says that when a fish swims by, the sea anemone injects venom into it by touching the fish with its tentacles. It then uses those tentacles to grab the fish and to pull it to its mouth so that it can consume the fish. Next, the professor mentions the oyster as an example of a marine animal that uses passive means to eat. The oyster doesn't hunt, so it simply filters water through its shell. It uses hairs that are on its body to grab nutrients like plankton, which it then eats.

Actual Test 03

Question 1

p. 21

Sample Answer 1

Agree

1 **turning in work late = get more time than others**
   - is similar to cheating
   - get an unfair advantage over classmates

2 **actions have consequences**
   - help students learn to finish work on time
   - ability will be helpful when have job in future

Sample Response

I fully agree with the statement. When students submit assignments late, teachers should lower their grades. For one thing, the due date is an important part of an assignment. All students must adhere to it, and students who turn in their work late benefit by getting more time than everyone else. That's similar to cheating because they're getting an unfair advantage over their classmates. For another thing, by punishing students by lowering their grades, teachers can show students that actions have consequences. They can hopefully help students learn to finish their work on time. That's an important ability which will come in handy for students in the future when they graduate from school and get jobs.

Sample Answer 2

Disagree

1 **students have too much homework**

- may be 1-2 days late
- unfair since other teachers give too much work

2 is discouraging
- late history report → -20%
- upset me → didn't want to work hard anymore

Sample Response

I understand why some teachers lower their students' grades when they turn in assignments late, but I don't think they should do it. First, many students have huge amounts of homework and simply can't cope with everything. I do my best at school, but I'm occasionally late with my work. I might turn it in one or two days late. It's unfair for teachers to lower my grades since the other teachers give me too much work to do. Second, it's discouraging when teachers lower your grades when you're late with assignments. Recently, I submitted a history report one day late. The teacher subtracted twenty percent from my overall grade. That really upset me and made me not want to work hard in his class anymore.

Question 2

Listening Script

Now listen to two students discussing the announcement.

W Student: Can you believe we have to write a paper about the play after we're done with it?

M Student: What's so bad about that?

W: I was hoping to spend the last month of school doing as little work as possible. Now, I have to write that paper instead.

M: Personally, I'm not really bothered by the assignment.

W: How come?

M: It seems like the assignment is meant for us to critique our performance. So I'll get a chance to analyze what I did and didn't do well. That way, I'll figure out exactly what I need to improve upon.

W: I never thought about it like that.

M: You should. By taking the time to contemplate your acting, you'll make fewer mistakes the next time you work on a play.

W: That's pretty clever, Kevin.

M: Thanks. Oh, yeah, and it's nice of the school to provide us with free tickets and transportation. Honestly, I could use the money I get from selling the tickets, and going there for free is better than paying for a taxi.

W: You can say that again.

Sample Answer

Reading Note

Students working on play → write 10-page paper on experience
- will get 3 free tickets → can sell for $15 each
- get free transportation to performing arts center

Listening Note

Man → wants to write paper

1 can critique performance
- can analyze what did well and badly
- figure out how to improve

2 likes free tickets and transportation
- wants money from selling tickets
- doesn't want to pay for taxi to center

Sample Response

The man and woman discuss the announcement by the Theater Department. It states that the students working on a play need to write a ten-page paper describing their role in the play and what they learned after it's done. In return, they'll get three free tickets and free transportation to and from the performance center. The man expresses his support for the announcement. He first points out that he doesn't mind doing the assignment. He believes it will give him a chance to evaluate his performance, which will help him improve and be a better actor in the future. He also likes the fact that he can sell the tickets since he says he could use the money. Finally, he appreciates the free transportation since that means he won't have to spend any money taking a taxi to get to the site of the performance.

Question 3

Listening Script

Now listen to a lecture on this topic in a botany class.

M Professor: People have long wondered if trees can communicate. Well, the first evidence supporting the notion of tree communication was discovered in the early 1980s. The initial clues came from studies done on willow trees that caterpillars had attacked. You see, uh, scientists noted that the trees underwent significant chemical changes to protect themselves. They also found the same chemical changes in nearby trees that had not been attacked. They concluded that, uh, somehow, the willow trees close to those under assault were being warned about the caterpillars.

Despite the evidence, the scientific community disputed the findings. But over time, more rigorous studies were conducted both in the field and in labs. The overwhelming evidence showed that trees really are capable of sending

Actual Test 03   **7**

chemical signals to one another when they're being attacked.

The obvious question is this . . . Why are the trees doing this? The answer is that it's most likely that the nearby trees are doing the equivalent of, uh, eavesdropping. When a tree in danger releases chemicals to protect itself, some of the chemicals spread so far that other trees pick them up by chance. So it's not exactly intentional communication between trees. It's more like, uh, someone reacting to danger and then everyone else seeing what's happening and acting in the same way.

Sample Answer

Reading Note

Tree Communication

trees → use chemicals to communicate w/other trees

- in danger → release chemicals
- other trees detect & protect themselves

insects may attack tree

- tree releases chemicals = leaves less tasty
- other trees detect → produce same chemicals

Listening Note

caterpillars attacked willow trees → trees protected selves

- nearby trees not attacked but still protected selves
- must have communicated somehow

trees eavesdropping

- released chemicals spread far
- other trees detect them → begin to protect selves

Sample Response

The professor tells the students about some studies that were done on willow trees. According to the studies, scientists learned that when caterpillars attacked willow trees, the trees began undergoing chemical changes to protect themselves from harm. The scientists also noticed that other willow trees which were not being attacked underwent the same chemical changes as the other trees. They concluded that the trees were somehow communicating with one another. The professor mentions that more evidence has been discovered showing that trees are able to communicate. This is related to tree communication, which is described in the reading passage. According to the reading, when trees release chemicals, they are detected by other trees located nearby. The trees then release the same chemicals in order to protect themselves from whatever is attacking the other trees. In that way, trees are able to communicate.

Question 4

Listening Script

Listen to part of a lecture in an astronomy class.

W Professor: Ever since ancient times, people have looked to the heavens and studied the stars and planets. Even in the distant past, people were able to utilize the knowledge they gained to reap a variety of benefits. Centuries ago, two of the most common ways people made use of astronomy were to make calendars and to navigate the seas.

The ancient Egyptians were able to create a calendar thanks to their observations of the skies. How did this help . . . ? Well, every year, the Nile River flooded. The floodwaters brought silt to the Nile River Valley, and the Egyptians used that fertile silt to grow the crops that allowed them to survive in the desert. One thing Egyptian astronomers realized was that the flooding happened annually during the summer solstice, which is in July. That was when the brightest star in the sky, named Sirius, rose before the sun did. Thanks to that knowledge, the Egyptians knew exactly when to expect the flooding and could therefore start preparing to plant their crops.

And what about navigation . . . ? The Vikings were among the best seafaring people in ancient times, and one reason was that they used astronomy to navigate their ships. They knew the concept of latitude, so they took measurements from the sun in the daytime and the star Polaris at night. If you don't know, Polaris is the name of the North Star and is located due north in the night sky. By measuring the angle between the sun or Polaris and the horizon, the Vikings knew which latitude they were at. This knowledge, uh, enabled them to navigate from their Scandinavian homelands to Iceland, Greenland, and other faraway places.

Sample Answer

Listening Note

Ancient people → used astronomy to benefit themselves

1 **Egyptians → created calendar from observing skies**
   - Nile River flooded every year → brought nutrients for farmers
   - knew when floods would happen → could prepare to plant crops

2 **Vikings → used astronomy to navigate**
   - knew about latitude → measured with sun and Polaris
   - could navigate to many places

Sample Response

The professor talks to the students about how people in ancient times used astronomy for their own benefit. She notes that two primary uses were for making calendars and for navigating on the ocean. Regarding the first benefit, she talks about astronomy in ancient Egypt. The professor says that the Nile River flooded and brought fertile silt to the Nile River Valley annually. The Egyptians studied the skies and learned that when the star Sirius rose before the sun, the floodwaters were coming. This knowledge of the calendar let them prepare to farm the land each year. The professor then talks about the Vikings. They knew about latitude, so they were able to use the location of the sun or the North Star to measure their latitude while they were sailing on the ocean. This knowledge enabled them to navigate their ships to distant lands such as Iceland and Greenland.

Actual Test 04

Question 1

p. 27

Sample Answer 1

Agree

1 **only need to know one subject**
   - students must know 5-6 subjects
   - not hard to learn one subject well

2 **teachers get more time off**
   - go home after school and do no work
   - have summer and winter vacations off

Sample Response

I find myself in agreement with the statement that it's easier to be a teacher than a student. For starters, teachers only have to be knowledgeable in one subject whereas students have to know at least five or six different subjects. It's not that hard to learn one subject very well in order to teach it, and that's all teachers need to do. Additionally, when the school day ends, teachers get to go home and relax while students must go home and study for several hours. Teachers also don't have to work during summer and winter vacations, but many students in my country spend several hours studying each day of vacation. Now that I think about it, being a teacher is much easier than being a student.

Sample Answer 2

Disagree

1 **end of school day**
   - students go home and do anything
   - teachers do grading for several hours

2 **preparation time**
   - teachers spend hours preparing lessons
   - students don't need to prepare much

Sample Response

I strongly disagree with the statement. Instead, it's my opinion that being a student is much easier than being a teacher. One reason concerns the amount of work both must do. In general, I finish my homework at school, so when the school day ends, I can go home and do whatever I want. On the other hand, teachers must often grade large numbers of homework assignments and tests after school ends, so they may work for several hours at night. Teachers also need to prepare their lessons before they teach them. This can take a few hours each day, especially if the teacher has classes in different grades. But students don't usually need to prepare for class other than by reading a few pages in their textbooks.

Question 2

p. 28

Listening Script

Now listen to two students discussing the announcement.

W Student: Huh. This is rather interesting. Can I assume you've seen the announcement about student-teaching as well?

M Student: Yeah, I already went to the office and signed up for a spot. I'm doing my student-teaching at a school located two minutes away from campus.

W: Lucky you. This announcement has really messed up my schedule. My mornings and afternoons are almost completely filled already.

M: How so? You aren't taking that many classes, are you?

W: I'm taking five courses this semester, but I also have a part-time job. I'm going to have to change my work hours now, and my boss won't appreciate that at all.

M: You'd better hurry and select a school as well. The good ones are getting snapped up quickly.

W: Yeah, and I might not get a good school. You know, I wish the school had made this announcement earlier.

M: Why do you say that?

W: Well, it's a great idea because it will give the students some really valuable experience doing student-teaching. We could use it. It's just that the timing of this announcement isn't very good.

Reading Note

Fine Arts Department juniors and seniors → must do student-teaching

- teach at elementary school or kindergarten
- once a week for 2 hours a day

Listening Note

Woman → has mixed feelings

1 **will mess up schedule**
   - 5 classes + part-time job
   - will have to change work hours

2 **thinks students will get valuable experience**
   - need experience
   - but timing isn't good → should have made announcement earlier

Sample Response

The woman has mixed feelings about the announcement by the Fine Arts Department. According to the announcement, juniors and seniors majoring in Fine Arts must do student-teaching at a local school. They have to do at least two hours of teaching one time a week. The woman tells the man about her feelings regarding the new regulation. To begin with, her schedule is already full in the mornings and afternoons due to her classes and part-time job. She comments that she will have to change her work schedule, which is going to make her boss displeased. However, she also speaks favorably about the decision because she believes that the students could use the experience that they'll get from doing student-teaching. She simply finds the timing of the announcement to be inappropriate. She points out that the announcement should have been made at an earlier time.

Question 3
p. 29

Listening Script

Now listen to a lecture on this topic in an environmental science class.

W Professor: One of the biggest dangers that coral reef ecosystems all around the world face is the overabundance of algae. Algae compete with coral for nutrients in the water, so, uh, if too many algae start growing, there won't be enough food for the coral, so the reef will die.

How do algae grow out of control . . . ? One major factor affecting algae growth is the presence—or lack of—large fish populations in a reef. Why is that . . . ? Well, many species of fish feed on algae and therefore keep the algae population in check. But if there's an environmental disaster,

such as an oil spill, this can cause problems. The oil kills many fish, which enables the algae to grow out of control. When that happens, the algae consume most of the food and thus put the coral in danger of dying.

Yet this usually does not happen. You see, um, coral reefs are attractive to marine life forms due to the abundance of life residing in them. As a result, most coral reefs prove to be quite resilient. New fish move in to replace the ones that died. These fish proceed to consume the algae, so the coral can remain alive. And that's how coral reefs can survive temporary algae growth blooms.

Reading Note

Resilient Ecosystems

ecosystem gets disturbed → heavily damaged
- many can overcome problems
- return to state of equilibrium → thrive again

Listening Note

environmental disaster in reef → oil spill
- many fish die
- algae grow out of control → consume food → coral in danger

coral reefs attract new life
- new fish move in
- consume algae → coral stay alive

Sample Response

During her lecture, the professor talks about coral reef ecosystems. She points out that they often have to deal with algae growing out of control. According to her, this can happen when there is an environmental problem such as an oil spill. Because of the oil spill, lots of fish might die. Since the fish eat the algae, when there are fewer fish, the algae can start growing out of control, which endangers the coral reef. Fortunately, coral reefs attract many fish, so new fish move into the area, and they start eating the algae, so the coral reef doesn't die. This is related to the concept of resilient ecosystems in that most ecosystems have ways to return to equilibrium. Thus even when the ecosystems are unbalanced, like coral reefs are when there are too many algae, the ecosystems can overcome the problem and return to their natural state.

Question 4
p. 30

Listening Script

Listen to part of a lecture in a botany class.

M Professor: For the most part, tropical plants live in humid jungle-like terrain at low elevations. However, in some parts of the world, high mountain ranges exist near the equator, so tropical plants can grow in these elevated regions. Some of these mountain ranges are found in, um, in Papua New Guinea and parts of South and Central America. At these high elevations, plants are subjected to extreme temperature changes in the course of a single day. 4,000 meters above sea level in the Andes Mountains, the temperature has been known to change from minus fifteen degrees Celsius to forty degrees above zero in fewer than twenty-four hours.

The primary issue for these tropical plants is dealing with frigid temperatures, uh, not extreme heat. The first method high-altitude tropical plants use is to maintain a cover of dead leaves on their stems. When the plants' leaves die, they don't fall off. At night, when the temperatures are the lowest, the living leaves bend inward and get covered by the dead leaves, which provide a layer of warmth for the plants' living parts. The frailjones flowering plant, which is common in the Andes Mountains in South America, has leaves which do this.

A second way plants protect themselves is by adapting to keep their internal water from turning to ice when the temperature drops below freezing. The water in these plants is drawn to their inner regions at night. The outer regions may freeze and form ice crystals, but this doesn't kill the plants since the freezing occurs outside their inner cells. Basically, um, these plants' outer regions may freeze and thaw every night, but they won't die.

Sample Answer

Listening Note

Tropical plants → adapt to live in high elevations

1 **use dead leaves as cover**
   - temperature falls at night → living leaves bend inward
   - covered by dead leaves = layer of warmth

2 **keep internal water from turning to ice**
   - draw water into internal regions
   - outer regions freeze but don't kill plants

Sample Response

The professor tells the students that there are some places near the equator with high elevations. As a result, the temperatures in these places can change from being extremely hot to very cold in one day. The plants living in these regions can handle the high heat, but they have had to adapt to be able to survive the frigid temperatures. One way they have done this is by retaining their leaves after they die. At night, when temperatures decline, the green leaves bend inward and get covered by the dead ones. The dead leaves help keep the other ones alive. The professor says the frailjones flowering plant in the Andes Mountains

does this. The second adaptation is that plants prevent their internal water from becoming ice. They draw their water to their inner parts, which do not get affected by low temperatures. This action keeps the plants from freezing and dying in cold weather.

Actual Test 05

Question 1   p. 33

Sample Answer 1

Agree

1 **spend hours playing games**
   - best friend got addicted → personality changed
   - are no longer friends

2 **develop bad habits**
   - may quit studying because of games
   - grades decline

Sample Response

I would have to agree with the statement that playing computer or video games has a negative effect on teenagers. I've noticed that many teenagers who play computer or video games frequently spend several hours a day playing them since they become addicted to them. One of my best friends became addicted to video games, and his personality changed considerably. He became so different that we quit hanging out and are no longer friends with each other. Teens who play these games also tend to develop bad habits. For instance, they often quit studying at school because they want to play games. I've seen several people neglect their studies in favor of computer and video games, and their grades declined severely as a result.

Sample Answer 2

Disagree

1 **can play games together**
   - learn about teamwork
   - get along w/others to succeed

2 **improve hand-eye coordination**
   - shooting games = reaction times improve
   - am more coordinated thanks to games

Sample Response

I don't think teenagers are harmed by playing computer or video games. In fact, I believe the opposite and feel that these games can help teenagers. For example, many games these days are ones which large numbers of people can play together. That means teens need to team up with other players in order to succeed in the games. Therefore, in the process of playing computer and video games, teens learn about teamwork and how to get along with others to achieve their goals. Secondly, many games help improve people's hand-eye coordination. I play some computer games, especially ones that involve shooting. I've noticed that my reaction times have improved tremendously and that I'm much more coordinated since I began playing them.

Question 2 p. 34

Listening Script

Now listen to two students discussing the letter.

M Student: You're close friends with Carla Gant, aren't you?

W Student: Yes, I am. Did you happen to read her letter to the editor in this morning's paper?

M: Yeah, I just finished reading it.

W: She makes some valid points, doesn't she?

M: Kind of . . . But I don't agree that the school needs to extend the break between classes.

W: Yeah? Why do you feel that way?

M: To be frank, uh, ten minutes is plenty of time to talk to a professor and to get to your next class. This campus isn't all that big, you know. And most professors are okay with students being three or four minutes late to class as well.

W: Hmm . . . Yeah, I suppose you're right.

M: Another point is that students can send email to their professors or visit them during their office hours. That's what I always do when I have a question. I especially love email. My professors are all quite good about responding to my emailed questions with thorough answers.

W: Perhaps Carla's experience hasn't been the same as yours.

M: You may be right. But I still don't think the change she wants is necessary.

Sample Answer

Reading Note

Not enough time in between classes

- should be 20 minutes instead of 10
- wanted to talk to profs → didn't have time

Listening Note

Man → disagrees w/letter writer

1 **10 minutes = enough time to talk**

- small campus → can get to classes quickly
- profs don't mind if 3-4 minutes late

2 **can email profs or visit them in office hours**
- can ask questions that way
- email is good → profs always respond

Sample Response

The man and woman discuss the letter to the editor in the school newspaper. The letter mentions that there isn't enough time in between classes for students to speak with their professors. So the letter writer requests that the school make the break in between classes be twenty minutes rather than ten. The man disagrees with the letter writer's opinion and believes that the break time doesn't need to be extended. His first argument points out that the campus is small, so it's possible for students to ask questions after class and to get to their next class on time. He adds that the professors don't mind if the students are a bit late to their classes. His second argument is that students can write emails or visit professors in their offices to ask questions. He notes that he is pleased by how his professors answer his questions by email.

Question 3 p. 35

Listening Script

Now listen to a lecture on this topic in a psychology class.

W Professor: When you're a teacher, it's important to know how to let students know why they're being punished when they misbehave. Let me tell you a story from my days teaching elementary school.

One year on the first day of school, I taught my first graders the class rules, including that they shouldn't draw or write on their desks and the walls. Well, this one girl, uh, Mary was her name . . . She simply didn't understand why she couldn't do that. She constantly drew on her desk and the walls with her crayons. I tried all sorts of punishments . . . I made her stand in the corner, but she enjoyed that. I kept her in the classroom during recess, but she didn't care about that either. Finally, I got so frustrated that I called her parents and told them to keep her home for a day.

Do you know what . . . ? That punishment actually worked. Mary finally realized how serious her actions were. Prior to that, the punishments weren't severe enough to dissuade her from misbehaving. But she really didn't want to miss school. That punishment hurt her. And she realized that she couldn't attend school if she wrote on her desk. I gave her that punishment one more time, but, after that, she stopped misbehaving and became a model student.

Reading Note

Logical Consequences

act in certain manner → specific results

- get caught breaking law → punished
- laws exist, so people aware of consequences
- punishment needs to be severe though

Listening Note

told students not to write on walls and desks

- Mary didn't follow rules
- punished many times → all punishments ineffective

told Mary's parents to keep her home for a day

- was effective punishment → didn't want to miss school
- stopped misbehaving & became model student

Sample Response

The professor talks about a time when she was a first grade teacher. She explained to her students that they shouldn't write on the desks or walls, but one student continually did that. When she made the student stand in the corner or stay in the classroom during recess, the student didn't care, so she kept writing on the desks and walls. Then, the professor told the student's parents that she couldn't attend school for a day. Because the student liked school, not being able to go hurt her. She realized she was behaving badly, so she quit writing on the desks and walls. The student's actions were related to logical consequences. This is the notion that certain actions have logical results. When illegal or improper actions are done, if the punishment is severe and known in advance, then a person, realizing the logical consequences of the action, will not do it.

Question 4 p. 36

Listening Script

Listen to part of a lecture in a zoology class.

W Professor: There's plenty of scientific evidence proving that when female mammals become mothers, they undergo, well, several changes. For example, um, they become braver and faster and develop better memories. Some of this evidence comes from a study done on rats. A series of tests were undertaken to examine the differences in behavior between rats that had babies and those that didn't. The tests were carried out for more than two years to prove that the ability lasted the entire lifetime of each of the mother rats.

One of the tests involved the rats getting through a maze. Time after time, the mother rats were able to find the food in the maze and did so at a faster rate than the other rats.

That proved they had better memories. In addition, the mother rats displayed more protective attitudes and bravery when facing various dangers. For example, um, instead of fleeing from danger like the rats that weren't mothers did, the mother rats typically confronted it and thereby showed a greater amount of fearlessness. A third test concerned the rats' hunting abilities. The mother rats consistently showed better skills at tracking down and killing crickets.

The researchers attributed this behavior to changes in the chemical makeup of the mother rats' brains. After the rats gave birth and began lactating, their brain chemistry was altered. This provided them with more flexibility in their behavior, which gave them an edge over the rats with no babies. One example of this change was that the mother rats' vision improved. This enabled them to find and capture prey more easily. Researchers are now investigating whether these changes are typical of all mammals, including humans.

Listening Note

Female mammals = change when become mothers

1 **mother rats got through maze faster**
   - showed had better memories
   - were more protective and braver and had better hunting skills

2 **chemical makeup of brains changed**
   - brain chemistry altered when lactating
   - gave more flexibility in behavior + vision improved

Sample Response

During her lecture, the professor talks about some changes that occurred in rats which had become mothers. The first changes she mentions concern how the mother rats behaved. For instance, they were able to get through a maze faster than rats that weren't mothers. They appeared to be braver than other rats since they didn't run away from danger but faced it instead. They had better hunting abilities than rats that weren't mothers, too. The professor also points out that as soon as the rats gave birth and began creating milk, their brains were physically altered. This caused them to develop more flexible behavior, and their eyesight got better as well. Their improved eyesight helped them capture prey much better. Essentially, the professor claims that because the rats had become mothers, they developed physical and mental characteristics better than those of rats which didn't have any young.

Actual Test 06

Question 1 p. 39

Sample Answer 1

Agree

1 **are young so are easy to control**
   - teachers clapped hands → students became quiet
   - was easy for teachers to teach

2 **elementary school students = eager to learn**
   - don't misbehave
   - listen closely

Sample Response

After thinking about the statement, I believe it's correct, so I agree that it's easier to teach students at elementary schools than students at universities. First, elementary school students are young, so they're easy for teachers to control. I remember when I was an elementary school student. All the teachers had to do to get our attention was clap their hands or turn off the lights. That made all of the students quiet, so then the teachers could easily teach us. In addition, most elementary school students are eager to learn, so they don't misbehave in class. Instead, they often listen closely and try to learn the various lessons the teachers are giving them.

Sample Answer 2

Disagree

1 **university students want to learn**
   - pay lots of money
   - don't waste $ by misbehaving

2 **know the value of education**
   - if learn more, can get good job
   - bro was good student → professors loved teaching him

Sample Response

I strongly disagree with the statement because I feel that university students are much easier to teach than elementary school students are. First of all, most university students are there because they want to learn. They pay lots of money in tuition each semester, so they keep quiet, act well, and don't misbehave. They don't want to waste their money, so they are very easy for university professors to teach. In addition, university students know the value of an education. They want to learn as much as they can so that they can get good jobs after they graduate. My brother always asked questions and did his homework on time. He was an outstanding university student, and all of his

Question 2 p. 40

professors loved teaching him.

Listening Script

Now listen to two students discussing the announcement.

W Student: Doug, have you read this flyer about the writing and research seminars the school is going to be holding?

M Student: I saw it, but I'm not particularly interested in it. I got good grades in high school, so I shouldn't have a problem here at college.

W: You ought to reconsider your opinion, Doug. We're only freshmen, and I'm sure our professors here have different expectations than our high school instructors did. I'm definitely going to attend some of the seminars to see what kinds of papers we're going to be expected to write.

M: Yeah . . . I sort of see your point.

W: There could be another benefit.

M: What?

W: If the seminars are small enough, we'll have the opportunity to interact closely with the professors who are teaching them. Getting to know a couple of professors might come in handy in the future, especially if we wind up taking any of their classes. Who knows? Uh, it might help us out in some way.

M: Good point. Let's call the number and find out what the schedule is.

Sample Answer

Reading Note

Seminars teaching writing and research skills

- freshmen encouraged to register
- will be taught by profs

Listening Note

Woman → interested in seminars

1 **wants to know expectations of profs**
   - is freshman → college papers different from high school papers
   - want to learn how to write for profs

2 **interact closely w/profs**
   - can get to know profs
   - helpful if take their classes later

Sample Response

The students discuss a flyer that they read. It notes that the school is going to be holding seminars on writing and research skills during the first three weeks of the semester. Freshmen are urged to go to at least two of the seminars, which will be taught by professors at the school. The woman expresses her support for the seminars and indicates she will attend a few of them. She tells the man two reasons she thinks the seminars will be beneficial. One, she wants to know what kind of writing the professors at the university expect from students. She states that their expectations will probably be different than those of her high school teachers. She also remarks that if the seminars are small, she can get to know the professors teaching them. The woman thinks that knowing them could be beneficial in the future.

Question 3

p. 41

Listening Script

Now listen to a lecture on this topic in a psychology class.

M Professor: Have you ever noticed that the better you know someone, the more poorly you sometimes communicate with that individual? This is called close communication bias. You read about it in your textbooks last night, but let me give you a personal example to make sure you understand.

Last week, I tried to arrange lunch with a couple of my colleagues, but all sorts of problems happened due to a lack of understanding. I wanted to have lunch with Professor Dinkins and Professor Carter. I've known Professor Dinkins for many years, but I just met Professor Carter this semester. I told Professor Carter the name of the restaurant and gave him detailed directions on how to get there. As for Professor Dinkins, I just gave him the name of the restaurant. We had eaten there once before, so I assumed that he remembered where it was.

What happened . . . ? Professor Carter arrived there on time, but Professor Dinkins was twenty minutes late. He said he couldn't find the restaurant because he couldn't recall where it was located. Of course, that was my fault because I hadn't bothered to ask him if he had remembered. I just thought he would know where to go, so I didn't say anything about its location.

Sample Answer

Reading Note

Close Communication Bias

know person well → may assume person doesn't need detailed explanation

- omit important details = lack of understanding
- may explain same thing in detail to strangers

Listening Note

arranged lunch with two colleagues

- knew one well but had just met the other

- gave detailed directions to new prof but only name of restaurant to friend

friend was late

- couldn't remember the location
- but other prof was on time

Sample Response

During his lecture, the professor tells the students about something that happened last week. He mentions that he wanted to have lunch at a restaurant with two other professors. He gave detailed directions to the professor he didn't know well. But he only told the other professor the name of the restaurant. The professor he didn't know well arrived at the restaurant on time while the other one was twenty minutes late. The professor had assumed that his friend would remember the location of the restaurant since they had eaten there before, but that professor couldn't recall its location. That was an example of close communication bias. When this happens, people who are familiar with others often assume that those people know information that they actually don't. As a result, they omit certain information, which can often result in confusion or misunderstandings.

Question 4

p. 42

Listening Script

Listen to part of a lecture in a zoology class.

M Professor: Insects live in a wide variety of environments, including in water. There are some that can float or walk on water. In fact, there's an entire family of insects, uh, called the gerridae family . . . That's G-E-R-R-I-D-A-E . . . Anyway, the members of the gerridae family can both float and walk on water. There are nearly, um, 2,000 insects in this family. Most reside in fresh water, but around ten percent of them live in salt water in the planet's oceans. Most of the insects in this family are called water striders. Their ability to float and walk on water is helped tremendously by their body composition and the principle known as surface tension.

Here's a picture of a water strider . . . I'm sure you've seen it before. Notice that it has a long, slender body . . . as well as long legs. These help distribute the insect's weight evenly on the surface of the water. Each leg also has thousands of tiny hairs per millimeter of leg space. These hairs aid it in floating on the water. Each leg has a special function as, uh, some are used for movement while others are used for steering on the water like a boat.

Now, uh, what about surface tension . . . ? On the surface of a body of water, there's a thin film created by the attraction of water molecules to one another. This causes a downward pull of the upper molecules by the lower one. Combined with gravity, this makes the surface of the water very taut. As a result, the lightweight water striders can both float and walk on the water. Here, uh, let's watch a video of a water strider in action . . .

Sample Answer

Listening Note

Gerridae family of insects → can float and walk on water

1 **water strider → has long, slender body + long legs**
   - distribute weight evenly
   - hairs on legs help it float

2 **surface tension → creates thin film on surface of water**
   - caused downward pull of upper molecules by lower ones
   - combines w/gravity → lets water strider walk on water

Sample Response

The professor tells the class that the insects which belong to the gerridae family are capable of both floating on water and walking on it. He mentions that there are around 2,000 insects in the family and that they are usually known as water striders. He shows the students a picture of a water strider and points out its long body and legs. According to the professor, both of them distribute the weight of the insect evenly. There are also thousands of hairs covering the water strider's legs. These two factors enable the water strider to float. As for walking on the water, the professor attributes this to surface tension. The combination of a thin film on the surface of water and gravity makes the surface of the water taut, so water striders, which are very lightweight, can effectively walk on the water.

Actual Test 07

Question 1
p. 45

Sample Answer 1

Talent

1 **cousin = outstanding musician**
   - has never taken music lessons → has natural talent
   - sings in popular band

2 **classmate = excellent artist**
   - picked up paintbrush and started painting
   - is good despite having no formal training

Sample Response

While it's possible for some people to become outstanding musicians or painters through training and hard work, it's much more important that they be talented. My cousin is an outstanding musician, but he's never taken a music lesson in his life. Instead, he simply has natural talent, which is something that can't be taught. He sings in a band that's becoming popular, and it's all thanks to his own ability. Additionally, one of my classmates is an excellent artist. One day, she simply picked up a paintbrush and began painting. She discovered that she was good at it despite never having any formal training. Today, she has a blog on which she posts some of her paintings, and it's somewhat popular since her artwork is so good.

Sample Answer 2

Training and Hard Work

1 **need years of training & hard work to succeed**
   - friend studies at art school
   - works hard & has good teachers → is considered top young artist

2 **hard workers = more determined to succeed**
   - talented but lazy singers = less popular
   - less-talented but hardworking singers = more popular

Sample Response

Being talented is nice, yet training and hard work are more important to succeed as a musician or painter. A person can do well with natural talent, but it takes years of training and hard work to attain real success. One of my friends attends an art school, where he studies painting. He has worked hard for years and has trained with many art teachers. Thanks to their help and his desire to succeed, he's considered a top young artist in my country. People who work hard are also usually more determined to succeed than those who try to get by on their talent. In my country's music industry, many talented but lazy singers are less popular and successful than less-talented singers who train and work very hard.

Question 2
p. 46

Listening Script

Now listen to two students discussing the article.

M Student: Can you believe the school administration is forcing Pete's Pizza to close? That's outrageous.

W Student: I don't see a problem with that. The owner is being greedy by refusing to pay his employees enough money.

M: You can't possibly be serious, can you?

W: Of course I am.

M: One of my friends works there. He is happy with his wages at the restaurant, and he says Pete's a great boss. He doesn't want more money, but the school is insisting that Pete pay higher wages.

W: That's right. He should do that.

M: Yeah, but . . . uh, now the restaurant is closing, so my friend and several other students are losing their jobs. They're not going to make any money at all.

W: Oh . . . yeah.

M: In addition, the school shouldn't tell Pete how to run his business. He's obeying all the laws, and that's the only thing which matters. If students think they aren't getting paid enough, they're welcome to find jobs elsewhere. That's how the free market is supposed to work, but the school is interfering with it.

Reading Note

Pete's Pizza will close

- rent has doubled
- school pressuring owner to double minimum wage

Listening Note

Man → upset restaurant is closing

1 **friend working there is happy w/wages**
   - doesn't want more $
   - is losing job → won't make any $ now

2 **school shouldn't tell Pete how to run business**
   - is obeying laws → that's important
   - students can work elsewhere if think they aren't making enough $

Sample Response

According to the article in the school newspaper, the restaurant Pete's Pizza is going to close after being on campus for many years. The owner of the restaurant says that the school has increased his rent and is also demanding that he pay his workers too much money. As a result, he can't make a profit. The man is very upset about the article because he believes the school is acting improperly. He states that one of his friends works at the restaurant and is satisfied with the money he earns. Unfortunately, because of the school, the restaurant is going to close, so his friend and the other student employees won't have jobs any more. The man also points out that the school is interfering with the free market. He remarks that students can choose whether or not they want to work there and that the school shouldn't get involved in the matter.

Listening Script

Now listen to a lecture on this topic in a zoology class.

M Professor: Let's look at dogs as an example of how people try to understand what animals are communicating to us. If you ask me, dogs' ears are a great place to start. As you are probably aware, most dogs' ears can, uh, stand up straight, move forward, and move backward, to name a few movements. And, um, as I discovered, these slight shifts have different meanings to dogs.

I frequently go for walks with my dog Pepper. Once while we were walking, Pepper saw a big truck speeding down the road toward us. His ears went straight up and forward, which I interpreted as meaning that he was afraid of the truck. I was certainly frightened, so I assumed Pepper felt the same way. But, uh, on a later occasion, I saw his ears go straight up and forward when he met another dog. Pepper and the other dog started growling at each other, so I realized that when his ears looked like that, he was signaling aggression, not fear.

Another time, Pepper suddenly pulled his ears back. I thought he wanted to play, so I picked up one of his toys. A few seconds later, I heard a noise coming from the backyard. Pepper started barking loudly and ran to the window. Apparently, he'd sensed someone in the backyard, so he was showing suspicion.

Reading Note

Animal Communication Problems

humans often can't understand animals

- minute change in signaling = means a lot to animals but not to humans
- frequently misinterpret animal's signaling

Listening Note

1 **dog's ears = straight up and forward**
   - thought the dog was frightened
   - later realized it meant aggression

2 **dog's ears = pulled back**
   - thought the dog wanted to play
   - actually was showing suspicion

Sample Response

The professor tells the class about a couple of incidents involving his dog Pepper. One time, when Pepper saw a truck driving toward them very quickly, his ears went up and forward. The man thought that Pepper was afraid since he was, but he saw Pepper do the same thing with his ears another time and then start growling at another dog. He realized he had misinterpreted the gesture, which really meant aggression. Later, Pepper pulled his ears back. The professor thought Pepper wanted to play, but the dog was actually showing suspicion. The professor's lecture is related to animal communication problems. Humans don't often notice small changes in how animals communicate despite the fact that these minor changes can have major meanings to animals. Humans also frequently misunderstand what animals are signaling, so they are unable to communicate well with animals.

Question 4

p. 48

Listening Script

Listen to part of a lecture in a zoology class.

M Professor: Wading birds, or waders, are birds that live along shorelines and in marshy regions. They're called waders because they, er, they wade in the water to find food. Egrets, herons, cranes, storks, spoonbills, and flamingoes are all waders. These birds typically live on fish, amphibians, reptiles, insects, invertebrates, and shellfish, which they find in shallow water and mud. When searching for food in muddy areas, waders rely upon two special adaptations.

The first of them is their bills, which are large and elongated. Look up here at the pictures of some of their bills on the screen . . . and you'll see what I mean. Now, uh, these bills are long for a reason. Simply put, uh, they enable waders to scoop fish and other food out of the water. The long bills also help waders dig into the mud to find food sources buried in it. Many species of waders have sensitive nerve endings at the ends of their bills. These nerve endings let them detect movement in the mud, so they can zero in on food sources buried within it.

The second adaptation is found in the feet and legs of waders. You see, uh, many waders have web-shaped feet. By this I mean that they have skin growths between their toes. The webbed shape of their feet helps them walk in soft mud, so they don't sink into it and get stuck. Additionally, their legs are quite flexible and allow them to bend over easily, so the birds can dip their bills into the mud and then scoop out whatever food they find. Thus they can feed themselves more easily thanks to their feet and legs.

Sample Answer

Listening Note

Waders → two adaptations for searching for food in muddy areas

1 **bills are large and elongated**

- can dig in mud to find food
- have sensitive nerve endings → can detect movement in mud

2 **web-shaped feet**

- can walk in mud easily → don't sink
- flexible legs → can bend over easily

Sample Response

The professor mentions that birds such as storks, egrets, and flamingoes are waders because they wade in shallow water, where they search for food. He lectures that these birds frequently look for food in mud and that they've adapted to be able to acquire food from muddy areas in two ways. The first adaptation concerns their bills. Waders have large and long bills. Thanks to the length of their bills, waders can dig in the mud to find food. Many waders also have nerve endings on their bills that are very sensitive, so they can locate animals moving in the mud. That lets waders find their food more easily. The feet and legs of waders let them effectively look for food in mud, too. The web-shaped feet of waders prevent them from sinking in mud while their flexible legs permit the birds to bend over easily while hunting for food in mud.

Actual Test 08

Question 1

p. 51

Sample Answer

Agree

1 **need to get knowledge and skills for future**

- will rely on them as adults
- if stop school, won't get good skillset

2 **can't get job if younger than 16**

- applied for part-time job when 14 → rejected
- companies won't hire young people full time

Sample Response

I agree that everyone should be required to attend school until they're sixteen years old. First of all, young people should attend school to acquire the knowledge and skills they'll rely upon when they're adults. If they stop attending school before they turn sixteen, they most likely won't develop a skillset that will enable them to be successful in the future. Next, if young people don't attend school, they need to find jobs to occupy their time. However, there are virtually no places willing to hire people fourteen or fifteen years old. When I applied for a part-time job at the age of fourteen, I was rejected for being too young. So that company and others like it definitely wouldn't hire a fourteen-year-old for full-time employment.

Sample Answer 2

Disagree

1 **some people = unfit for school**
   - don't want to learn or don't get along w/others
   - boy in bro's class → never did schoolwork → should have let him drop out

2 **some jobs = don't require schooling**
   - father's classmates dropped out to become farmers
   - similar students should be able to quit school

Sample Response

I don't believe everyone should be forced to attend school until they're sixteen years of age. One reason is that some people are simply unfit for school. Perhaps they don't want to learn, or maybe they don't get along well with others. But these individuals shouldn't be forced to attend school if they don't want to. A boy in my brother's class absolutely hated school and never studied or did any homework. He should have been allowed to drop out since he wasn't doing anything productive at school. Additionally, some people will do jobs that don't require schooling. When my father was younger, many students at his school dropped out because they were going to be farmers. Students like my father's classmates shouldn't have to stay in school either.

Question 2

p. 52

Listening Script

Now listen to two students discussing the letter.

W Student: Check out this letter to the editor. Can you believe it?

M Student: Are you talking about the guy who wants to get rid of all the TVs in the dorm lounges?

W: Yeah. I've got a couple of opinions regarding this letter.

M: I'd say he makes some good points in the letter.

W: I partially agree, yet I also disagree.

M: What do you disagree about?

W: To begin with, he wrote that students don't talk to each other that much because of the TVs. On the contrary, the students in my dorm often watch news programs in the lounge. Then, when the programs conclude, we discuss what we just saw. We've had some really enlightening conversations after watching TV together.

M: That's interesting. So, uh, how do you agree with the

letter writer?

W: Some people watch too much television, so they neglect their studies. Even if they're watching educational programs and are, uh, therefore learning, they still need to do their homework. So it sort of makes sense to remove the TVs as well.

M: Those are a couple of good points you made.

Sample Answer

Reading Note

School should remove TVs in dorm lounges

- students watch TV → neglect studies
- don't communicate w/others
- too noisy → disturb others

Listening Note

Woman → has mixed feelings regarding letter

1 **students in dorm watch news programs**
   - discuss news w/others
   - have had good conversations

2 **students watch too much TV**
   - neglect studies
   - need to do homework

Sample Response

The letter to the editor that the students are talking about requests that the school remove the televisions which are in the lounges in the school dormitory. The letter writer claims that the TVs make students study less, cause them not to know their neighbors, and are so noisy that they disturb others. The woman tells the man that she sees both sides of the argument, so she has mixed feelings. To oppose the letter writer's opinion, she gives an example from her own life. She says that she and the other students in her dorm watch news programs and then have discussions about them after they end. However, she recognizes that some students watch too much television and therefore don't do all of their studies. As a result, they cannot complete some of their assignments. In that regard, she supports the letter writer's opinion.

Question 3

p. 53

Listening Script

Now listen to a lecture on this topic in a biology class.

W Professor: One method some spiders employ to attract prey is to use pheromones. The many different species of bolas spiders, which reside in South America, Africa, and Asia, are capable of doing this quite successfully. What they do is reproduce the sexual pheromones of female moths to attract male moths.

Interestingly, only the female bolas spider has this ability. And each species of female bolas spider can produce a pheromone for only one or, uh, a few, specific species of moths. So the spider is unable to lure all types of moths. Here's what happens . . . A chemical signal is emitted by a female spider, and soon, uh, a male moth detects the signal and is attracted to it. Why? Well, the signal indicates to the male that a female is ready to mate. When the moth follows the chemical signal, it comes into the bolas spider's range.

The female bolas spider has an unusual method of capturing its prey. It extends a line of web, and, uh, at the end is a blob of web that's extremely sticky. The spider swings the line at a moth and tries to snag it. It's almost as if the spider is, uh, fishing. While this may seem difficult, the spider is quite adept at it and manages to capture many moths this way.

Sample Answer

Reading Note
Fake Signaling
predator sends signal that prey can't resist
- prey follows signal to source
- prey then attacked by predator

Listening Note

bolas spider → reproduces sexual pheromones of female moths
- male moth detects signal → attracted to it
- follows signal → moves into spider's range

spider catches moths w/web
- swings web at moth and tries to snag it
- like it is fishing

Sample Response

The professor lectures to the class about the female bolas spider, which has a unique method of attracting and capturing prey. The female bolas spider can release a pheromone that is identical to that of a female moth when she is ready to mate. The pheromone proceeds to attract male moths, which then fly to where the spider is waiting. The spider uses a line of web with a really sticky blob of web at the end. It then casts the line at the moth and tries to catch it with the web. The female bolas spider uses fake signaling in order to capture its prey. Fake signaling involves the sending out of a chemical signal by a predator to try to catch prey. The signal it emits is one that the prey cannot resist, so the prey winds up going right to where the predator is waiting for it.

Question 4

p. 54

Listening Script

Listen to part of a lecture in an environmental science class.

W Professor: Most people would agree that floods have negative results. After all, they can cause property damage, kill people and animals, and displace others. Nevertheless, floods are sometimes regarded in a different light. Some people, um, farmers in particular, consider them beneficial. Why? Well, there are two main advantages of floods for farmers: Floods replenish the soil with nutrients . . . and they provide water during arid times.

People have been aware of the first benefit since ancient times. In Mesopotamia and Egypt, two of the world's first civilizations, numerous people lived alongside flood plains. Each year, the rivers would rise, flood the land, and cover it with silt that was full of nutrients. When the water receded, farmers planted their crops in the rich soil, which, uh, which ensured that the people would have food during the following year. The people in these civilizations believed the annual floods were gifts from the gods rather than disasters. On the contrary, a year in which there was no flooding . . . or in which there was less flooding than usual . . . was considered a disaster. Interesting, huh? Even today, farmers residing in regions with poor irrigation or fertilizing methods benefit from floods in the same manner.

The second advantage is that floodwaters can be trapped and saved for future use. By digging artificial ponds, farmers can retain large amounts of water after the flooding recedes. During the growing season, farmers can pump the water out of these ponds to ensure that their crops get a sufficient amount of it. This is a necessary procedure in places with dry seasons and is particularly useful for crops such as rice, which requires a great amount of water to grow.

Sample Answer

Listening Note
Are some benefits to floods
1 **Mesopotamia and Egypt → depended on floods for farmland**
- floodwater brought rich silt
- planted crops in land w/silt → fed people w/crops

2 **trapped floodwater**
- dug artificial ponds → retain water when flooding ends
- use water in ponds for crops

Sample Response

While lecturing, the professor tells the students that even though most people believe flooding has disadvantages, some people believe it can also provide certain benefits. She describes two reasons that people such as farmers feel this way. The first reason is that flooding can provide soil with nutrients. As far back as ancient Mesopotamia and Egypt, people were aware of this advantage. When the rivers in those areas flooded each year, they deposited silt rich in nutrients, on the land. The farmers planted their crops in the silt and grew enough food to feed people. According to the professor, people in those cultures considered a year with little or no flooding to be a bad one. Next, the professor states that people can create artificial ponds to trap floodwaters. This is useful in dry lands that get little water because the farmers can use the water they keep to irrigate their crops during the growing season.

Actual Test 09

Question 1

p. 57

Sample Answer 1

Agree

1 **modern art = awful**
   - create very ugly works
   - spatter paint on canvas and call it art

2 **musicians = mostly pop music**
   - may be popular but are soon forgotten
   - no importance to society

Sample Response

I agree that artists and musicians aren't important to society. First of all, if you look at the state of modern art, you'll be completely disgusted by it. Artists in the past tried to create beautiful paintings, drawings, sculptures, and other works, but modern artists seem to try to create the ugliest works possible. Other artists simply spatter paint on canvas and call that art. I fail to see how society benefits from their work. The same is true of musicians nowadays. The music that gets the most airplay is pop music. The people who sing the songs are popular one day and forgotten the next. While some of their music may be entertaining, it surely has no importance to society.

Sample Answer 2

Disagree

1 **beautiful art made in the past**
   - Renaissance and Impressionist artists
   - helped define their societies

2 **musicians also helped societies**
   - Bach, Mozart, and Beethoven
   - other modern musicians = important

Sample Response

I disagree with the statement because I believe artists and musicians are very important to society. When I think of European society, images of the beautiful art created by Renaissance masters and nineteenth-century Impressionists come to mind. The works those artists created defined their societies, so they were of great importance to it. The same is true of musicians. Consider musicians such as Bach, Mozart, and Beethoven. The European societies they lived in benefitted immensely from their compositions. The same can be said for many other musicians living around the world in the present time. Without artists and musicians, societies would be much different than they currently are, and that difference would cause these societies to be lessened in their greatness.

Question 2

p. 58

Listening Script

Now listen to two students discussing the letter.

M Student: You know, uh, this letter writer has a point about all the littering on campus. But I don't think the solution he proposes would work.

W Student: Actually, I believe it would be rather effective.

M: Why do you say that?

W: My city had a huge littering problem a couple of years ago. So the city council passed a law that fined people $20 for littering. You wouldn't believe how quickly people stopped throwing their trash on the ground.

M: Seriously? Did your city start looking better?

W: It sure did. And I believe the same thing would happen here if we used the student's solution.

M: That would be great. There really is a lot of trash on the ground.

W: Oh, another thing is that the school would save money. After all, uh, it would need fewer groundskeepers and janitors to pick up the litter that everyone's creating. And, of course, the school would make money from the students it fines. I hope the school administration seriously considers implementing his suggestion.

Sample Answer

Reading Note

Too many students littering

- should fine students $15 for littering

- will decrease littering + make campus more beautiful

Listening Note

Woman → agrees with proposal

1 **city had littering problem**
   - fined people $20 for littering
   - people stopped littering quickly

2 **would save school $**
   - need fewer workers to clean up litter
   - school would make $ from fines

Sample Response

The student who wrote the letter to the editor requests that the school do something about the littering problem it is facing. The writer believes that one way to solve the problem would be for the school to fine students $15 every time that they litter. The woman and man discuss the contents of the letter, and the woman tells the man that the writer's proposal should be effective. She tells the man about how her city did something similar a few years ago. It fined people who littered $20, and that caused the littering problem to go away very quickly. She also remarks that the school could save money because it would need to hire fewer people to clean up all of the litter. As an additional bonus, the school would make money from the fines that it collects from students who get caught littering.

Question 3

p. 59

Listening Script

Now listen to a lecture on this topic in a marketing class.

M Professor: Nowadays, many movies are promoted through the use of teaser advertisements. Sometimes these ads are done for movie franchises that people are familiar with, but they can also be used effectively for movies that no one knows much about. Let me give you an example of each . . .

Star Wars is one of the best-known film franchises in the world. The *Star Wars* movies have made billions of dollars since the first film was released in 1977. Well, the creators of *Star Wars* are brilliant at using simple and short ads to promote the films. They show well-known characters from the films or action, such as light saber fights or flying spaceships, to create excitement for the movies months ahead of their release dates.

Another film that used teasers with great success was the 1996 film *Independence Day*. I remember watching some of the teasers. I knew that aliens were going to invade the Earth. I knew the White House was going to get destroyed. But I didn't know much else. I simply had to see that movie on opening night. *Independence Day* went on to become, at

that time, the second highest grossing film of all time, and it was the teaser ads that helped make it such a success.

Sample Answer

Reading Note

Teaser Advertising

short ad → prepares public for larger ad campaign + product launch
- used for films, TV shows, and computer games
- may be a few seconds long
- provides small glimpse of product

Listening Note

1 *Star Wars* = **successful film franchise**
   - simple and short ads promote films
   - show well-known characters or actions → create excitement

2 *Independence Day* = **1996 movie**
   - saw teasers → knew aliens invaded but not much else
   - had to see movie on opening night → was very successful film

Sample Response

The professor lectures to the students about the movie franchise *Star Wars* and the movie *Independence Day*. He mentions that there are short and simple ads for *Star Wars* months before each movie is released. The ads often show characters or action people are familiar with, so they get people excited for the films. He also points out that the ads for *Independence Day* were extremely successful. They divulged that aliens would attack the Earth and destroy the White House, but they didn't tell much else. That got people interested in the film, so it became highly successful. Those movies were successful thanks in part to teaser advertising. Teasers are short ads which provide a bit of information about a new product, especially a movie, TV show, or computer game. Teasers get the public excited about the new product and can help increase sales.

Question 4

p. 60

Listening Script

Listen to part of a lecture in a marketing class.

M Professor: In the business world, demand refers to the desire of consumers for a certain product. There are two types of demands: primary and secondary. Primary demand is for a type of product as a whole. For instance, um, there's a demand for computers in general. Secondary demand is for a specific brand-name product. So, uh, people need computers, and they want, um . . . computers manufactured by the XYZ Corporation. Let's look at how advertisers deal with these two types of demands.

Primary demand advertising focuses on the positive aspects of a product in general. Surely you've seen ads on TV for the beef industry or for milk products. Did you notice that these ads don't name any specific brands . . . ?
Instead, uh, they just tell consumers that beef and milk are healthy foods and that they should purchase those products. Many times, primary demand advertisements are paid for by large lobbying groups working for certain industries. Basically, the people in those industries pay lobbyists to promote their products.

Now, uh, secondary advertising targets specific brand names. This is the more common kind of advertising. Companies hire ad agencies to make ads to sell their products. We're bombarded by these types of ads on a daily basis. They can be ads for individual products such as, oh, Coca-Cola and Pepsi. They can be ads for restaurants such as Burger King and McDonald's. And they can be ads for companies such as Microsoft and Apple. In each case, the brand name is emphasized, so consumers are encouraged to purchase specific products.

Sample Answer

Listening Note

Two types of advertising → primary and secondary demand advertising

1 **primary demand advertising → advertise product in general**
   - ads for beef and milk → no brands mentioned
   - paid for by lobbyists working for industries

2 **secondary demand advertising › specific brand names**
   - companies hire ad agencies to sell products
   - ads for products, restaurants, companies, and others

Sample Response

According to the professor, there are two types of demand. Primary demand refers to the demand for a certain kind of product while secondary demand refers to the demand for a specific brand name. The professor notes that there are different ways that these products are advertised. Regarding primary demand advertising, it doesn't mention any company names but instead focuses on a product in general. The professor mentions ads for the beef and milk industries. Ads for them simply encourage people to buy beef and milk but don't single out any companies. As for secondary demand advertising, it consists of ads that mention actual brands. The professor says that these ads are more common, and he mentions ads for companies such as Coca-Cola, Burger King, and Apple. The brand

names of the products being sold in secondary demand advertising are given so that customers can purchase specific items.

Actual Test 10

Question 1
p. 63

Sample Answer 1

Taking Notes during Lectures

1 **need to write down material for tests**
   - help me prepare
   - almost always get A's

2 **understand material better**
   - can't write down everything teachers say
   - must understand important info → write that down

Sample Response

When I'm in a class, I take comprehensive notes on what the teacher says. For me, that's much better than listening without taking any notes. To begin with, I have to know what the teacher is saying to learn the material and to study it later when I'm going to take an exam. Since I take excellent notes, I just need to study them to prepare for my tests, and I almost always get A's. I also feel that taking notes helps me understand the material my teachers are discussing. Since I can't write every word the teachers say, I have to understand exactly what they're talking about to write down the important information. And when I do that, I understand the material better.

Sample Answer 2

Listening to Teachers without Taking Any Notes

1 **teachers lecture on info in book**
   - when study, just go over books
   - can do fine on tests

2 **have terrible handwriting**
   - used to take notes → couldn't read on writing
   - wasted time trying to understand what I wrote

Sample Response

Although my friends prefer to take notes in their classes, my style is to listen to my teachers without taking any notes. One reason is that almost all of my teachers lecture only on the information in the textbooks. So if I want to study for my exams, all I have to do is read my schoolbooks, and I can do fine on my tests. Another reason is that I have terrible handwriting. I used to take notes, but when I went back to read them, I found that I could barely read my own writing. It took me a long time to figure out what I had written. I wound up wasting too much time, so I quit taking notes and focused on listening closely to my teachers.

Question 2 p. 64

Listening Script

Now listen to two students discussing the announcement.

M Student: Oh, I'm so excited about this announcement.

W Student: What? The thing about the book?

M: Yeah, that. I've got two papers in mind, so I have to think hard about which one to submit. Aren't you going to turn one in?

W: Me? No way. Writing isn't my forte, so it would be a waste of time for me to enter the contest.

M: Well, I'm going to, and I'm pleased the school is doing this.

W: Why is that?

M: First, it's a chance for fifteen students to get published. That will help their résumés out a considerable amount, especially if they intend to go to graduate school.

W: Yeah, you're right. I hadn't thought about that.

M: Another thing is that it will give students a chance to read some excellent papers. I mean, uh, I might learn a few things by reading the winners' papers.

W: Well, best of luck to you, Pierre. I hope your paper gets chosen.

M: Thanks for the kind words. I appreciate them.

Sample Answer

Reading Note

Students can submit work to be published

- top 15 papers will get published
- will be selected by profs

Listening Note

Man → likes the announcement

1 **chance for 15 students to get published**
   - will help résumés
   - will be good if go to grad school

2 **will give students chance to read excellent papers**
   - might learn from reading papers

The man gives his opinion of the announcement by the dean of students. According to it, the school is going to hold a contest to select the top fifteen academic papers from the past year. Then, the papers are going to be published in a hardcover book before the school year ends. The man thinks this is a great idea and is very excited about the possibility of one of his papers being selected. He tells the woman two reasons why he supports it. The first one is that it will let fifteen students have their work published. He points out that it will look good on their résumés and might help them get into graduate school. The second one is that he will get a chance to read some good papers that other students wrote. He believes he might learn something by reading these papers.

Question 3 p. 65

Listening Script

Now listen to a lecture on this topic in a marketing class.

M Professor: How to move slow-selling merchandise is one of the biggest problems for businesses. As a general rule, the most expensive products are the hardest to sell. But there's a way to get rid of them . . . Businesses simply make a newer, yet more expensive, model of the product they want to sell.

Let me give you an example . . . Hmm . . . Imagine that your company manufactures coffeemakers. You've got three models . . . One sells for fifty dollars, another for seventy-five, and the last one for a hundred. The seventy-five-dollar model is your biggest seller because most consumers make compromises. They don't want the cheapest or most expensive model, so they purchase the one in the middle.

But you've got lots of coffeemakers priced at one hundred dollars, and you want to sell them. Here's what you do . . . You introduce a new coffeemaker that sells for one hundred fifty dollars. Suddenly, the machine selling for one hundred dollars doesn't look too expensive, does it . . . ? Shoppers figure that it must be good, and it's not too costly when they compare its price with that of the newest model. When shoppers buy it, they see themselves as making a compromise. So, uh, even though they're spending more money, they don't believe they're spending too much. After all, they're not buying the most expensive model, are they?

Sample Answer

Reading Note

Compromise Effect

shoppers compromise and buy item that isn't too cheap or too expensive

- businesses offer higher-priced items
- shoppers buy items that were once most expensive →
  now regard as reasonably priced

Listening

company sells 3 coffeemaker models
- sell for $50, $75, and $100
- bestseller is $75 model

want to sell $100 coffeemakers
- introduce new model → sells for $150
- $100 model looks good now → shoppers will buy it

Sample Response

The professor tells the students about a way a company that sells coffeemakers can sell its most expensive products. He has the students imagine that a company offers three coffeemakers at three different prices. He states that the one priced in the middle sells the best. However, the company wants to get rid of its high-priced coffeemakers. So what it does is that it introduces a fourth coffeemaker which is more expensive than all the other ones. When people notice it, they start to purchase what used to be the most expensive coffeemaker. Since it is no longer the highest-priced model, customers don't think they're spending too much money. Their actions are an example of the compromise effect. Most people don't want to purchase the cheapest or most expensive item. Instead, they get an average-priced item. So companies introduce more expensive items to induce shoppers to spend more money on their products.

Question 4

p. 66

Listening Script

Listen to part of a lecture in a physiology class.

W Professor: It sure is cold today, isn't it . . . ? I believe it's ten degrees below zero right now. Well, this cold weather has gotten me thinking about how humans can survive such frigid temperatures. You know, uh, by using common sense, most people can manage to live through even the coldest weather on the planet. The two basic principles are to stay warm however you can and to make sure you have enough food.

There are three essential ways to stay warm. First, wear plenty of clothing and wear it in layers so that you can remove some if it gets too warm. Be sure to wear a hat, too. You lose around forty percent of your body heat through your head, so a hat can help your body retain heat. And wear warm gloves and good boots, or you may get frostbite on your fingers or toes. Second, stay indoors as much as possible. A good shelter will keep you out of the wind, which can reduce the temperature considerably. Third, have a fire or some other source of external heat to provide warmth.

Remember that your body requires food as well though. You need food and drinks to keep your body's inner core temperature up so that you don't get hypothermia. That's a state in which your body's core temperature falls too low . . . below thirty-five degrees Celsius. If you don't get your internal temperature back up, you'll die. Food and drinks can do that, and they'll provide you with energy. You may not realize this, but the body burns a lot of energy trying to stay warm in cold temperatures. Without ample food, you'll never survive.

Sample Answer

Listening Note

Humans → can survive extremely cold weather

1 **three ways to stay warm**
   - wear many layers of clothes
   - stay indoors → keep out of wind
   - have fire or other heat source

2 **body needs food and drink**
   - can avoid getting hypothermia
   - body burns lots of energy staying warm → need ample food

Sample Response

The professor comments that it is possible for people to survive very cold temperatures by following two main principles. They are to stay warm and to get enough food. The professor gives three tips on how to stay warm. First, people should wear enough clothing, including hats, gloves, and boots, to keep from getting cold and to retain body heat. Next, they should stay indoors to keep out of the wind. Last, they should have an external heat source such as a fire. The other way a person can survive cold temperatures is to consume lots of food and drinks. The professor says that the body expends a great amount of energy to stay warm and that energy can be provided by food and drinks. By having food and drinks, a person can make sure his or her internal temperature doesn't get too low, which could be fatal.

Actual Test 11

Question 1

p. 69

Sample Answer 1

Work in Another City

1 **have moved several times in past**
   - enjoy moving
   - new places and people

2 **making more $ = attractive option**
   - need $ to buy many things
   - don't mind moving for more $

Sample Response

If I had to make a choice between the two options, I would select the first one. Firstly, I have moved several times in my life, so moving again wouldn't be a problem for me. In fact, I actually enjoy moving because I get to experience new places and meet new people. Secondly, making more money is an attractive option for me. These days, it's important to earn as much money as possible. I need money to get a nice home, a car, clothes, food, and all of the other necessities of life. So I would gladly choose any job that paid me more money even if I had to move to another city to take that job.

Sample Answer 2

Work in My Current City

1 **live with elderly parents**
   - take care of them
   - don't want to move out of their house

2 **am not motivated by $**
   - is nice to have
   - but isn't decisive factor when choosing job

Sample Response

It would be nice to make more money, but I would take the second choice and remain in the city in which I currently live. I live with my parents, both of whom are getting old. As their only child, I believe it's my duty to take care of my parents in their old age since they helped me so much in my youth. As a result, I have no desire to move out of their house, so I wouldn't be interested in moving to another city. I also am not motivated by money. Yes, it's nice to have money, but how much money I will earn is not the decisive factor when I'm trying to decide where to live and work.

Question 2

p. 70

Listening Script

Now listen to two students discussing the announcement.

W Student: It's about time. The school has needed to crack down on those people for the longest time.

M Student: What are you talking about? This decision by the administration is horrible.

W: I disagree. I got sick after I ate a hotdog at a football game last month, and I don't want anyone else to suffer like I did.

M: The school administration is being too heavy handed with this ruling. I mean, uh, it's just one or two people selling bad food, but now everyone on campus is going to get punished for their misdeeds.

W: But this is the only way the school can keep us safe.

M: Sorry, Jenny, but you're wrong.

W: I don't think so.

M: Oh, and here's another point. You're in the Music Department, right?

W: Uh, yes. What does that have to do with anything?

M: At those concerts your department puts on, students sell concessions at them, right . . . ? Do you know that the money they make goes to buy new equipment and other things for the Music Department? Oh, well. Tough luck. Students don't get to sell concessions anymore.

W: Hey . . . I never realized that.

Sample Answer

Reading Note

Students & student groups → can't sell concessions at student events

- sell substandard & expired items
- students have gotten sick

Listening Note

Man → disagrees w/decision

1 **school is heavy handed**
   - only a couple of people selling bad food
   - school is punishing everyone

2 **Music Department students can't sell concessions now**
   - use $ raised to buy new equipment
   - but can't raise $ anymore

Sample Response

The man and woman have an argument about the announcement made by the school administration.

According to the announcement, students and student organizations have been selling bad food at school-sponsored events, so people have gotten sick. As a result, students and student groups are no longer allowed to sell food to students on campus. The man believes that this policy is misguided. He claims that there are only a small number of students or groups selling bad food. However, the school is not singling out those people but is instead punishing everyone. He also points out to the woman that students sell concessions in order to raise money for their departments. He says that due to the ruling, the Music Department, which the woman is in, won't be able to sell concessions and to buy equipment with the profits any longer.

Question 3

Listening Script

Now listen to a lecture on this topic in a physics class.

W Professor: Over the weekend, I read an article in a nature magazine that described the effects of ship noise on whales. As we covered in a previous lecture, whales use sound to communicate with one another, to find food, and, uh, to navigate in the ocean. They do this by sending out sound waves. Unfortunately, the number of ships on the world's oceans is so great that the sounds of the ships' propellers, engines, and sonars are causing serious disruptions to the lives of whales.

Essentially, uh, the whales' vocalizations are being masked by the noise created by these ships. One study done on killer whales showed that every increase of one decibel of noise from ships caused the whales to increase their vocalizations by one decibel to compensate. Ultimately, a threshold was reached where the killer whales couldn't make their vocalizations any louder, so they were masked by the louder sounds of the ships.

There are numerous negative results when this sound masking occurs. For example, uh, the whales' ability to find food can be reduced . . . The communication between whales that's essential for mating gets disrupted . . . And some experts speculate that whales beach themselves when the amount of noise made by ships becomes so great that they lose the ability to navigate properly.

Sample Answer

Reading Note

Sound Masking

one sound reduces person's ability to hear something else

- can use pleasing sounds to cover unpleasant ones

- negative results → airplane sounds mask TV
- artificial noises can harm some animals

Listening Note

killer whales' vocalization masked by noise from ships

- 1 decibel increase in noise → whales increased sounds by 1 decibel
- reached threshold → couldn't make vocalizations louder = sounds masked by ships

negative results

- ability get food reduced
- communication for mating disrupted
- some whales beach selves → maybe because of ship noise = can't navigate

Sample Response

The professor mentions to the students that the number of ships creating artificial noise on the world's oceans has increased to such an extent that it's having negative effects on the lives of whales. She mentions a study that was done on killer whales. Researchers noticed that the whales increased their vocalizations by one decibel each time the artificial noise also increased by one decibel. However, at some point, the whales couldn't vocalize any louder, so their sounds were masked. This had negative results, such as keeping the whales from finding food and disrupting their attempts at mating. Some people further believe that all of the noise may be causing whales to beach themselves. The whales' actions are related to sound masking because their sounds are being masked by other ones. As the reading passage notes, sound masking can have negative effects on many animals.

Question 4

Listening Script

Listen to part of a lecture in a zoology class.

M Professor: Animals typically live alone, in small groups, or in large groups, uh, called packs or herds. There are advantages and disadvantages to each type of lifestyle, yet it seems that living in large groups has more benefits than living in small groups or living a solitary existence. Interestingly, there are advantages for both predators and prey animals living together.

Two well-known examples of predators that live in packs are lions and wolves. Both are highly social animals, and the pack members almost always belong to the same family. For them, the primary benefit to living in a pack is hunting. Lions hunt in groups, which enables them to chase, corner, and attack large prey and then take it down. Lion packs may attack massive water buffaloes, large hippos, giraffes,

Actual Test 11 27

and even small elephants. Wolves also hunt in big packs and can kill huge elk and bison by attacking from all sides at once. Killing large prey results in more food for the pack, which is an obvious advantage.

Now, uh, what about prey animals . . . ? Large numbers of prey animals live in groups which we typically refer to as herds. The herd acts as a defensive force to protect its members, particularly the young. Water buffalo in Africa are known to act together to fight off lions and other predators to protect members that have been attacked. Zebras are another good example. They travel in herds to confuse predators. Their stripes act as a sort of camouflage because they make each zebra blend in with the rest. Therefore, none stands out and gets chosen to be attacked by predators.

Sample Answer

Listening Note

Animals living in groups → have advantages

1 **predators → lions and wolves**
  - hunt in groups → can take down large animals
  - get more food for pack

2 **prey animals → live in herds**
  - can defend itself from predators
  - water buffalo and zebras

Sample Response

At the start of his lecture, the professor mentions that animals which live in large groups typically gain more benefits than animals living in smaller groups or by themselves. Both predators and prey animals can benefit by living in large groups. The professor discusses predators first and uses lions and wolves as examples. He points out that both animals hunt in large packs. Because they hunt together, lions can kill water buffaloes and hippos while wolves can kill elk and bison. By killing these big animals, they can get more meat for all of the pack members. As for prey animals, the professor comments that they can be protected by living in large herds. Water buffalo can protect their young from predators and may even fight predators such as lions. Zebras take advantage of their stripes, which make it hard for predators to single out individual zebras to attack when they're in herds.

Actual Test 12

Question 1
p. 75

Sample Answer 1

Seeing It Alone

1 **can focus on movie when alone**
  - friends talk during movie
  - is disturbing

2 **can see movie when want to**
  - go with group → coordinate each person's schedule
  - have to see movie at inconvenient time

Sample Response

I've been to numerous movies, and I always prefer to see them alone. One of the reasons I feel this way is that when I'm by myself, I can focus on the movie. Every time I see a movie with my friends, they talk to me during the film. That really disturbs me, so I try to make sure I see movies by myself when I go to the theater. A second reason I feel this way is that I like being able to see a movie exactly when I want to. If you go with a group of people, you have to coordinate each person's schedule, so the time you see the movie is frequently inconvenient. By going alone, I don't have to deal with that issue though.

Sample Answer 2

Seeing It in a Group

1 **more fun w/group**
  - saw concert w/6 friends
  - had great time

2 **talk about movie or concert later**
  - discuss past events attended together
  - still talking about concert from 2 weeks ago

Sample Response

I love going to both movies and concerts in groups. To begin with, it's always more fun to go with a group of people than to go by yourself. A couple of weeks ago, I attended a concert with six of my friends. We had a great time at the concert since we all loved the band that was performing. In addition, when you see a movie or concert with other people, you have something you can talk about with them later. My friends and I often discuss what happened at concerts or during movies we saw together in the past. For example, we've been talking about the concert we saw two weeks ago nearly every day since we attended it.

Question 2

p. 76

Listening Script

Now listen to two students discussing the letter.

M Student: Ginny, you live in Weston Hall. Is the student who wrote this letter to the editor right?

W Student: Oh, yeah. You wouldn't believe how annoying it is having to live there. If I had known about the situation with the electrical outlets, I would have requested to live in another dorm.

M: It can't be that bad, can it?

W: I'm not exaggerating. My roommate and I constantly have to unplug appliances and then plug in others depending on which ones we want to use. That's a complete waste of time, and it's rather bothersome.

M: I bet it is.

W: The refrigerator has to stay plugged in at all times, so we only have two plugs to use for around, oh, ten other items.

M: That's terrible. I had no idea.

W: Yeah, and the RAs check students' rooms on occasion to see if they're using multi-plug outlets. If any students get caught, they get fined $100. That's so unfair.

M: You're telling me. I can't believe how bad that is.

Sample Answer

Reading Note

Not enough electrical outlets in dorm rooms

- room has two outlets
- students have many electrical appliances
- multi-plug outlets banned

Listening Note

Woman → agrees w/letter writer

1 **must unplug and plug in appliances**
   - plug in depending on what need to use
   - waste of time + bothersome

2 **RAs check students' rooms**
   - look for students using multi-plug outlets
   - catch students → $100 fine

Sample Response

According to the writer of the letter, there is a problem regarding a dormitory that was recently renovated. The dorm rooms have a limited number of electrical outlets, and the students staying in the rooms are not permitted to use multi-plug outlets. The woman agrees with the writer of the letter and tells the man that the situation there is terrible. She lives in that dormitory, and she says she and her roommate have about ten electrical items that they have to

keep plugging in and unplugging depending on which items they want to use. She comments that it's both a waste of time and annoying. She also claims that the RAs in the dorm enforce the ban on multi-plug outlets. They periodically check the students' rooms and fine them $100 if they are using the banned outlets in their dorm rooms. She believes it's very unfair to do that.

Question 3

p. 77

Listening Script

Now listen to a lecture on this topic in a management class.

M Professor: My family and I recently suffered from the Abilene Paradox. Let me tell you what happened so that you can understand precisely what it is.

Last weekend, my family went to dinner at a restaurant an hour's drive away from our home. The food was horrible, and we had a bad time at the restaurant and on the drive there and back. When we got home, I complained. Suddenly, my wife said she hadn't even wanted to go there. I asked her why she didn't say that before we left, but she responded that she had thought everyone else wanted to go, so, uh, she didn't want to upset us. Then, uh, my son added that he had felt the same way, but, like his mother, he didn't want to be the only person to say he didn't want to go there.

Honestly, I really hadn't wanted to go out either. My wife had commented about not wanting to cook dinner, so I had assumed she was hinting she wanted to eat out. Personally, I would have preferred to order a pizza. But I had thought she and my son wanted to eat out, so I suggested the restaurant. The next time, I'll ask for everyone's honest opinion so that we don't suffer through another incidence of the Abilene Paradox.

Sample Answer

Reading Note

The Abilene Paradox

all members of group don't want to do something

- believe others want to do it → feel pressure to go along
- don't voice negative opinion → would upset group dynamics
- if one person expresses disinterest, others would, too → could avoid doing activity

Listening Note

went to restaurant → had a bad time

- wife and son said didn't want to go
- neither wanted to say anything though

prof didn't want to go either
- prof just wanted to order pizza
- suggested restaurant since though wife and son wanted to go out

The professor discusses an experience he went through with his family that involved the Abilene Paradox. According to the reading passage, the Abilene Paradox happens when none of the members of a group wants to do something but each of them believes the others want to do that particular activity. Because they don't want to ruin the fun for everyone else, they all keep quiet and don't express their desire not to do the activity. This is exactly what happened to the professor and his family. He believed his wife wanted to eat at a restaurant, so he suggested going out for dinner. They had a bad meal and trip to the restaurant, and when they got home, they all mentioned that they hadn't wanted to go out in the first place. However, each of them had thought the others had wanted to eat out, so they didn't say anything.

Question 4

p. 78

Listening Script

Listen to part of a lecture in a zoology class.

W Professor: Most animals defend their territory vigorously against any intrusions by animals of their own species. After all, their territory is the place they consider their home, and it's also where they acquire their food. However, there are some instances in which animals permit their territory to be violated by members of their own species. Let me tell you about two of them . . .

The most common reason an animal would permit another into its territory is mating. This is especially true for species that don't bond for life. Two examples of these animals are the cheetah and leopard. Males and females get together only to mate. Uh, otherwise, they maintain separate territories. During the mating season, males and females seek one another and can safely cross into other animals' territories without being attacked. Female and male leopards stay together for several days while mating, but then they go their separate ways and must again be careful about not violating another animal's territory.

A second reason animals may permit territorial invasions is what's known as the, um, dear enemy recognition factor. This is a case in which the animal encroaching upon the territory is not a complete stranger but is instead recognized by the other animal. Two animals with adjacent territories may know each other well, so they're sometimes willing to permit minor territorial transgressions and won't act

aggressively. They are, essentially, dear enemies. What does that mean . . . ? Well, hmm . . . they're not exactly friends, but they're not enemies that will attack on sight. However, if a stranger—uh, an unknown animal, that is—enters the territory, the defender doesn't know its intentions, so that animal will act aggressively to protect its land.

Listening Note

Animals may permit territorial violations by members of own species

1 **mating = most common reason**
   - cheetah and leopard → don't bond for life
   - seek others during mating season → can violate territory

2 **dear enemy recognition factor**
   - encroaching animal isn't stranger to other
   - may live in adjacent territory → allow minor transgressions

At the start of her lecture, the professor stresses the importance of territory to animals since that's their home and the place where they find their food. She says that most animals will attack other animals of the same species that invade their territory on sight. However, she notes that there are some exceptions. She then talks about two of them. The first exception happens due to mating. During the mating season, animals may cross into territory belonging to others and not get attacked. This is particularly true for animals such as cheetahs and leopards, which live alone when they're not mating. The second exception happens when two animals are familiar with each other. The professor calls this the dear enemy recognition factor. Essentially, the animals have adjoining territories, and they know each other by sight, so they won't immediately attack if one of them enters the other's territory.

Actual Test 13

Question 1

p. 81

Sample Answer 1

Agree

1 **live in small town → nice people**
   - shopkeepers know name
   - ask for directions → get polite response

2 **big city people = rude and mean**
   - asked for help → people ignored me
   - were so impolite

Sample Response

It's definitely true that people in small towns are nicer than people in big cities. I currently live in a fairly small town, and most of the people here are quite nice. The shopkeepers all know my name, and even random pedestrians on the streets are kind to people. If you stop a person on the street to ask for directions in my town, the person will politely provide you with assistance. On the other hand, I've visited some of the big cities in my country, and the people there are simply rude and mean. I tried asking people for help, but everyone ignored me and walked right past me. I couldn't believe how impolite they were.

Sample Answer 2

Disagree

1 **live in capital → millions of people**
   - people in apartment complex = nice
   - workers at shops and restaurants = kind

2 **countryside → mean people**
   - was surprised
   - thought country people were nice

Sample Response

I disagree with the statement because I have had plenty of experiences with kind people in big cities and mean people in small towns. I live in my nation's capital, which has several million people. The people in my apartment complex are all nice to one another, and many workers at shops and restaurants are kind, too. In fact, they have to be nice because if they aren't, customers will visit other stores and restaurants since there are so many options. I've been to the countryside in my country several times, and I've encountered numerous mean people there. In fact, I was surprised because I'd heard that people in rural areas are generally nice. That, however, wasn't my experience.

Question 2

p. 82

Listening Script

Now listen to two students discussing the announcement.

M Student: This is awesome. I can't wait to join the new art club.

W Student: I'm sorry, but did you just say that you're going to join an art club? Aren't you an engineering major?

M: What? Engineers can't appreciate art?

W: I'm sorry. You're right. You just don't seem like, er, like the artistic type.

M: Well, I haven't gone to any galleries in the city yet because the prices are too high, but the fifty-percent discount is a great incentive. I won't mind paying $10 or $15 to get to the opportunity to admire priceless works of art.

W: Yeah, the city has lots of museums and galleries. It would be nice to visit them.

M: Totally.

W: So why else are you joining the club?

M: I'm mostly self-taught in art, so I'd like to hang out with people who are, um, trained in art. If I can learn from them, it will help me appreciate masterpieces even more.

W: I like the way you think. I may join as well.

M: You should. Let's do it together.

Sample Answer

Reading Note

New art club being established

- will focus on art appreciation
- members get 50% off admission to museums and galleries

Listening Note

Man → wants to join the art club

1 **hasn't visited galleries yet**
   - prices too high
   - 50% = great incentive

2 **wants to meet people trained in art**
   - is self-taught in art
   - wants to learn from others → can appreciate masterpieces more

Sample Response

The man and woman discuss the man's interest in joining the new art club that is going to form. The announcement mentions that the purpose of the art club will be to appreciate art, so the members are going to visit lots of museums and art galleries. As a benefit of membership, they will get into those places at half off the regular price. The man is eager to join the art club because he says he enjoys art. He comments that he hasn't gone to any museums or galleries because of the high price of admission, but he is willing to visit them for half price. He also remarks that he wants to spend time with people who know about art so that he can learn from them. Since he is self-taught in art, he wants to learn from people who are more knowledgeable than he is.

Question 3 p. 83

Listening Script

Now listen to a lecture on this topic in a psychology class.

M Professor: When studying history, one of the worst things we can do is oversimplify what we're studying. In many cases, important historical events don't happen for a single reason. Instead, they nearly always happen because of several different factors. Let me give you a couple of examples . . .

Hmm . . . Ah, here's one. In 1775, the American Revolution started. Now, uh, many people say that the colonists were tired of high taxes, so they revolted against the British. Well, um, there's some element of truth in that, but there were more issues than just taxes. Let's see . . . The colonists wanted representation in the British Parliament, they didn't want British soldiers in their homes and cities, and they wanted more autonomy. There were also unfortunate events such as the Boston Massacre, which ultimately led to the revolution.

The same is true of World War II. It didn't start merely because the Germans wanted to seize land from neighboring countries. What happened . . . ? Well, there were feelings of anger and resentment by the German people regarding how they were treated after World War I . . . There was the reluctance of Britain and France to stop German territorial ambitions when they had the chance . . . There was also the poor global economy at that time. Basically, numerous factors—not one thing—led to the onset of war.

Sample Answer

Reading Note

Oversimplification

explain something in basic terms → true meaning is lost
- oversimplify to allow for brevity → avoid going into detail
- if rush explanation or reduce detail, will be misunderstandings

Listening Note

1 **American Revolution**
   - most say started from high taxes
   - but were more issues
   - wanted representation in Parliament, no soldiers in homes, and more autonomy

2 **World War II**
   - didn't start just because of Germans seizing land
   - feelings of anger and resentment, other countries didn't stop Germany, and poor global economy

Sample Response

The professor lectures to the students about the American Revolution and World War II. He says many people give simple answers for why both wars started. Then, he notes there were several reasons that they began. Regarding the American Revolution, he points out that the colonists were not just unhappy about high taxes. Instead, they had many grievances, including a lack of political representation and the presence of too many British soldiers. Those issues as well as events such as the Boston Massacre led to war. As for World War II, it didn't happen only because the Germans wanted to seize land from their neighbors. It also happened because the German people thought they were treated badly and there was a poor global economy. The common explanations for the wars are related to oversimplification. This happens when people give a simple explanation for an event despite the fact that there are multiple factors involved.

Question 4 p. 84

Listening Script

Listen to part of a lecture in a zoology class.

M Professor: Something I'm sure nearly all of you have seen this fall is flocks of birds heading south. In the Northern Hemisphere, this happens every fall. However, prior to migrating, the birds need to prepare for their long journeys. There are two important activities they must do prior to departure. First, they need to store energy in the form of fat. Second, they have to molt so that they're in top condition for flying.

Essentially, birds must eat a great amount of food to put on fat before migrating. That will ensure they have a sufficient amount of energy to survive the trip. How much do they eat . . . ? Well, the garden warbler can double—yes, double—its weight from around eighteen grams to thirty-seven grams prior to migrating. It burns roughly three or four grams for each 1,000 kilometers it flies. Other birds experience similar weight gains. To compensate for their increased weight, which may hinder flight, the internal organs of many species of birds shrink. This ensures that they're light enough to fly and have enough energy.

Most migratory birds also molt before departing. By molting, um, I mean the removing of old feathers and the growing of new ones. Molting can involve just a few feathers or, uh, all of them. Replacing them requires a lot of energy, so it's typically done before migration. For example, the lazuli bunting, a bird that lives in western North America, molts in the fall before flying south to its winter breeding grounds in Mexico. By molting, the birds can be sure to have the best feathers for flying.

Sample Answer

Listening Note

Bird preparations before migrating south for winter

1 **eat lots of food → put on fat**
 - have enough energy to survive → may double body weight
 - internal organs shrink → keeps birds light enough to fly

2 **molting → removing old feathers and growing new ones**
 - uses lots of energy so is done before migration
 - gives birds best feathers for flying

Sample Response

The professor states that before birds migrate south for the winter, they have to do two important activities to prepare for their long journeys. First, they need to put on fat to store energy. Second, they need to molt. Discussing the putting on of fat, the professor points out that birds can use fat as energy while they're flying. According to him, some birds can double their weight. He mentions the garden warbler, a bird that can go from eighteen to thirty-seven grams in weight as it prepares to migrate. The professor also says that the internal organs of birds become smaller so that they can be light enough to fly due to their increased weight. Next, the professor discusses molting, which happens when birds lose old feathers and grow new ones. Molting requires energy, so birds molt before they depart. It also guarantees that they'll be flying with new feathers rather than old ones.

Question 1
p. 87

Sample Answer 1

An Interesting Class with a Strict Professor

1 **interesting class = pay close attention**
 - attend school to learn
 - pay more attention in interesting classes

2 **strict = beneficial**
 - many profs not strict → want to be friends w/students
 - students don't have to do homework + can cheat
 - want strict prof who doesn't let students be bad

Sample Response

If I were attending summer school, I would prefer to take an interesting class with a strict professor. The primary reason to attend class is to learn, and I can pay close attention if the class is interesting. When I am at school, I always learn more in interesting classes since I want to know the material. I also consider being strict to be a beneficial trait for professors. These days, too many professors are not strict at all. They want to be friends with the students, so they let their students get away with doing no homework or even cheating on tests. I want a strict professor who won't put up with the bad actions of any students. In my opinion, that's the best way to learn.

Sample Answer 2

A Class in My Major with an Average Professor

1 **summer school classes = intensive**
 - take class in major since familiar w/subject
 - sister took summer school → did better in major classes

2 **can still learn w/average prof**
 - pay attention in class + do reading
 - form study group → teach selves material prof doesn't cover

Sample Response

Of the three choices, I would prefer to take a class in my major with an average professor. First, summer school classes are intensive so can be difficult. Therefore, I'd prefer to take a class in my major since it would be a subject I'm familiar with. My sister took summer school classes before and always did better when taking classes in her major. In addition, if I have an average professor, I can still learn. All I have to do is pay attention during the lectures and do all of the reading. I can also form a study group with some other students. In that way, we can teach ourselves some of the material we don't learn in class since the professor is merely average.

Question 2

p. 88

Listening Script

Now listen to two students discussing the announcement.

W Student: Eric Carlyle? What a terrible choice for our graduation speaker.

M Student: What's wrong with Eric Carlyle?

W: I don't think he's worthy of being the speaker at graduation. He doesn't care enough about social issues.

M: On the contrary, I think he's an ideal person to speak at our graduation.

W: Why on earth would you possibly think that?

M: First, he's a graduate of our school. I think it's wonderful when the school gets fellow alumni to give speeches here. After all, these people shared many of the same experiences as us, so they know exactly how we're feeling as we graduate.

W: Hmm . . . But still . . .

M: And here's something else.

W: What?

M: When Eric Carlyle attended school here, he had nothing. He came from a poor family, but he worked hard and became the successful businessman he is today. It's nice to know that you don't need to be rich or have connections to be successful. His life story inspires me to try my hardest to be as successful as him. And that makes him a perfect choice to speak at graduation.

Sample Answer

Reading Note

Eric Carlyle → will be speaker at graduation ceremony

- multibillionaire businessman
- got rich in several different industries

Listening Note

Man → agrees w/choice of speaker

1 **is graduate of school**
   - likes when alumni give speeches
   - have shared experiences

2 **Carlyle came from poor family**
   - worked hard and became successful
   - life story = inspiring

Sample Response

According to the announcement, the school has gotten a wealthy businessman named Eric Carlyle to speak at its upcoming graduation ceremony. Mr. Carlyle graduated from City University many years ago and went on to become highly successful in three different fields of business. The man fully supports the school's choice of Mr. Carlyle as the graduation speaker. He gives the woman two reasons he likes the choice. The first reason is that Mr. Carlyle graduated from their school. He thinks Mr. Carlyle therefore has a connection with the graduating students since he was in their exact situation many years ago. He also says that the story of Mr. Carlyle's life is inspiring to him. Mr. Carlyle was once poor, but he worked hard and became a billionaire. The man believes that the way Mr. Carlyle became successful makes him a great choice to be the graduation speaker.

Question 3

p. 89

Listening Script

Now listen to a lecture on this topic in a psychology class.

W Professor: Hiding our true feelings isn't easy. After all, we want to laugh when we're amused, cry when we're sad, and, um, shout for joy when we're happy. However, the rules of society tell us that we should not always express our emotions. Instead, we occasionally have to manage them to hide our true feelings.

Let me tell you a story . . . I used to work in an office with another woman who was, well, extremely bossy. She wasn't a manager, but she always tried ordering me around. I simply hated working with her. Well, one day, she got fired. I was so happy I felt like jumping for joy. Unfortunately, everyone else in the office was very sympathetic to her and expressed their sadness.

What did I do . . . ? I put on a sad face like everyone else. I mentioned how unfair it was that she had gotten fired since she was such a good worker. Was that the truth? Absolutely not. But I couldn't tell her that she had deserved to get fired and that I was happy about it. That would have upset all of my colleagues, and it would have made me look heartless. So I managed my emotions and didn't smile until I was far away from my workplace.

Sample Answer

Reading Note

Impression Management

may need to manage facial expressions → avoid upsetting others

- feel happy when other person has misfortune

- can't express joy → will upset others
- so must have neutral or sympathetic expression

Listening Note

bossy woman at office got fired

- hated working with her → was happy she got fired
- others in office sympathetic = expressed sadness

put on sad face like others

- said was unfair was fired
- wasn't truth but couldn't say she deserved to be fired
- managed emotions until later

Sample Response

The professor points out that it's sometimes necessary for people to hide their true feelings from others. She says that when she used to work in an office, there was a very bossy woman who always gave her orders despite not being the professor's boss. The professor couldn't stand that woman. When that woman got fired, the professor became very happy. However, she couldn't express her true feelings since her colleagues were being sympathetic to the woman. The professor then masked her feelings by making a sad face and telling the woman how unfair it was that she had gotten fired. She didn't want to smile in front of the woman and her colleagues since that would have upset them and made her look bad. What the professor did was an example of impression management. It refers to a time when an individual must manage his or her facial expressions to keep from upsetting others.

Question 4

p. 90

Listening Script

Listen to part of a lecture in a theater class.

W Professor: Now that we've examined the various types of theater productions, I'd like to look at the concept of the fourth wall as it relates to the theater. In case you don't know, the fourth wall refers to the, um, the invisible wall between the audience and the stage. Think of a stage as a box with the background scenery and sides of the stage serving as three walls. The fourth wall is the one in front of the stage and therefore between the actors and audience.

In most stage productions, the performers act as though the audience isn't there. The audience merely observes the stage and the action taking place on it. The actors, in turn, ignore the reactions of the audience and perform as if they were alone. The audience, however, may be aware of information certain actors don't know, which heightens the drama or humor of the production.

On occasion, actors break the fourth wall. When doing this, they look at the audience and speak directly to them. Some

actors even run into the audience and give them things or ask them to participate in the play in some manner. This is called breaking the fourth wall. It's as old as the theater itself. In ancient Greek plays, the chorus spoke or sang to the audience to provide information regarding the setting or time. In many of William Shakespeare's plays, the actors give asides to the audience during which they make witty remarks about another character or situation. As a general rule, breaking the fourth wall is more typical of comedies than other types of productions.

Sample Answer

Listening Note

Fourth wall between actors and audience

1 **performers ignore fourth wall**
   - audience observes acting on stage
   - may be aware of info some actors don't know

2 **breaking the fourth wall → speak to audience**
   - Greek plays → chorus spoke or sang to audience
   - Shakespeare's plays → actors give asides

Sample Response

The professor lectures that the fourth wall is the invisible wall located between the stage and the audience. She remarks that there are two ways in which performers act with regard to the fourth wall. The first way is for the performers to ignore the fourth wall. They simply act like the audience is not watching the performance even when the audience reacts to the action in some manner. The second way is for the performers to break the fourth wall. When this occurs, they interact with the audience in some way. They may speak to or run into the audience, give things to audience members, or ask the audience to participate in the performance. The professor mentions that plays performed in ancient Greece broke the fourth wall as do plays written by William Shakespeare. According to her, it's more common in comedies than in other types of plays.

Actual Test 15

Question 1

p. 93

Sample Answer 1

Agree

1 **don't want government involved**
   - government should be small

- shouldn't spend taxpayers' $

2 private individuals and organizations = can help better
- many people help endangered animals
- should encourage more people to help

There are many endangered animals in my country, but I agree with the statement that the government shouldn't spend any money to protect them. First, I don't think the government should get involved in this sort of matter. I believe the government should be as small as possible and shouldn't spend taxpayers' money on matters such as this. Another thing is that I believe private individuals and organizations would do a much better job of protecting endangered animals than the government ever would. I've seen stories on the Internet about private individuals helping endangered animals such as elephants and tigers. We should encourage more people like them to provide assistance rather than beg the government to get involved.

Sample Answer 2

Disagree

1 set aside large areas of land for animals
- would cost a lot
- only government can afford

2 have responsibility to protect animals
- don't want more animals to go extinct
- government should spend $ to keep them alive

I disagree with the statement because I believe the government ought to spend as much money as necessary to protect endangered animals. For example, the government could set aside large areas of land to protect various endangered species in my country. That would require a great amount of money, and only the government could afford to do that. In addition, we have a responsibility to protect the animals in our country and on the entire planet. Too many species have already gone extinct, so the government ought to spend enough money to save these animals and to keep them alive. I don't want to see any more animals in my country going extinct because that could have negative consequences on the environment in the future.

Question 2

p. 94

Listening Script

Now listen to two students discussing the announcement.

M Student: Mika, weren't you enrolled in the English class that just got canceled?

W Student: Yeah, that was the one I was taking. I'm so depressed by what happened.

M: Yeah, I'm sorry to hear that.

W: To be honest, I'm not merely sad about it. I'm also rather upset with the school for canceling it.

M: But there weren't enough students enrolled in it. How can they, uh, break the rule?

W: That rule gets broken all the time. In fact, there are two other classes in the English Department which have fewer than ten students in them, but neither of them has been canceled.

M: That can't be right. Are you sure?

W: Of course I'm sure. I'm currently enrolled in one of them.

M: Oh . . . Well, uh, why don't you take the Renaissance poetry class at Richardson College?

W: Um . . . Do you realize that Richardson College is located an hour away from here? I don't own a car, and neither does anyone else in the class. How would any of us get there?

M: Er . . . I have no idea.

Reading Note

Poetry class canceled

- not enough students enrolled
- students can cross-enroll in similar class at other college

Listening Note

Woman → upset by class cancellation

1 classes can have fewer than 10 students
- says are 2 other classes with fewer than 10 students
- is taking one of them → hasn't been canceled

2 can't go to Richardson College
- is an hour away
- doesn't own car → doesn't know how could get there

The announcement by the English Department mentions that a class being taught on Renaissance poetry has been canceled because there are only seven students enrolled in it. There need to be ten or more students for the class not to be canceled. The announcement encourages the students to take a similar class at another college which is located close to the school. The woman is very displeased with the announcement. She points out that the school does not always follow the rule that there must be ten or more students in a class. She claims she's in another class with fewer than ten students, but it hasn't been canceled. So she thinks the Renaissance poetry class shouldn't have been canceled either. She also states that Richardson College is an hour away. None of the students in the class has a car, so she doesn't know how she could get to that school.

Question 3

p. 95

Listening Script

Now listen to a lecture on this topic in a psychology class.

M Professor: I hate speaking in public . . . That may sound strange coming from a professor, but now that I've been teaching for twenty years, I've gotten used to it. Nevertheless, when I first started teaching, I was almost always a nervous wreck. On some occasions, I became physically sick before I gave a lecture, especially if it was on a topic I wasn't very familiar with.

Then, I learned about defensive pessimism and began overcoming my fears. Here's what I did . . . I focused on everything that might go wrong during my lecture. For instance . . . What if the projector broke down? What if I forgot my notes? What if a student asked a question I couldn't answer? The list of potential problems I came up with went on and on. After all, there were numerous things that could have ruined my lectures.

What I discovered was that I became so focused on preparing my lectures and thinking of solutions to potential problems that my fears were greatly reduced. By the time class began, I was calm and completely prepared for anything. Now, uh, since you have class presentations next week, some of you might be feeling a bit anxious about them. Well, to be as prepared as possible, consider what might go wrong and find solutions ahead of time. Then, you'll be fine.

Sample Answer

Reading Note

Defensive Pessimism

think of negative things that could happen

- can plan for every eventuality
- helps people deal w/anxiety
- channel energy to solving problems

Listening Note

hates speaking in public → used to get sick before lectures

- focused on what could go wrong in lecture
- came up w/list of potential problems

focused on thinking of solutions to potential problems

- fears were reduced
- was calm and prepared for class

Sample Response

The professor declares that he hates speaking in public and that he often got physically sick prior to giving lectures when he was a new teacher. He mentions that he learned to get over his fears by focusing on what problems could potentially happen. For example, the projector could break, students could ask hard questions, or he could lose his notes. As he thought about these problems and how to solve them, he realized that his fear of public speaking was going away. In fact, he was calm and prepared for class when it was time to lecture. The professor's actions show how he used defensive pessimism. This happens when people think of all the negative things that could happen before they do something and then consider how to solve these problems. By focusing on these possible issues, people can lessen their feelings of anxiety and overcome their fears.

Question 4

p. 96

Listening Script

Listen to part of a lecture in a marine biology class.

M Professor: Many species of river fish, including salmon and trout, make long migrations during their lifetimes. Yet rivers have obstacles such as rapids and dams. Rapids appear when a riverbed is steep, which causes a great increase in the flow rate of the water. Dams, of course, are built across rivers to harness their energy to make electricity. Despite these two obstacles, fish typically manage to travel upriver and downriver. How do they do it . . . ?

Well, their bodies enable them to negotiate rapids in most cases. Swimming downstream is usually not a big deal since the fish merely go with the flow of the river. Traveling upstream, on the other hand, can be a problem. Still, fish have evolved over time to manage rapids. Salmon, for instance, have incredibly strong bodies enabling them to leap up to four meters at a time. By leaping out of the water in stages, they can negotiate rapids and reach calmer waters.

Obviously, uh, dams can't be leaped. Recognizing this problem, people build fish ladders around dams to assist the fish in bypassing them. In general, a fish ladder has a series of pools. The fish can leap to the first pool, rest, and then leap into the next one. Eventually, they can enter the river above the dam. Unfortunately, not all fish complete their journeys upstream. Some get sucked into the turbines of dams while others miss the fish ladder entrances. Even more don't have enough energy to negotiate either the rapids or fish ladders. Nevertheless, enough manage to get upstream and to reproduce to ensure the survival of their species.

Listening Note

Obstacles in rivers blocking fish moving up and downriver

1 **bodies can negotiate rapids**
 - easy to move downstream
 - upstream = salmon can leap four meters → leap out of water in stages

2 **dams block rivers**
 - fish ladders = let fish move past dams
 - not always successful → some fish can't get past turbines or over fish ladders

Sample Response

The professor tells the students that some fish, such as salmon and trout, migrate long distances during their lifetimes. As they swim downriver and upriver, they often have to get past both rapids and dams. Fish usually don't have a problem going through rapids when they're heading downriver, but swimming upriver can be more problematic. Fish such as salmon have developed strong bodies though. They can leap up to four meters out of the water, so that's how they get past rapids. Since fish can't leap over dams, people build fish ladders to help them get upriver. A fish ladder has a series of pools. The fish leap from one pool to the next and eventually reach the top of the dam. Not all fish manage to get past the rapids and dams, but enough of them do so that they can reproduce and keep their species alive.

Actual Test 16

Question 1 p. 99

Sample Answer 1

Go Alone

1 **spend time looking at artwork**
 - go with others → hurry through exhibits
 - go alone → admire paintings as long as want

2 **don't want others to talk to me**
 - contemplate paintings & how artists created
 - go alone → no one disturbs me

Sample Response

If I were planning to visit an art gallery, I'd prefer to go by myself. One reason I'd do that is that I could spend as much time looking at the artwork as I wanted. In the past, I went to galleries with friends and family members. They often wanted to hurry through the exhibits while I preferred to stop and look at them. By going alone, I would be able to admire each painting for several minutes if I desired. A second reason is that when I look at artwork, I don't want anyone to talk to me. I would rather spend time contemplating the paintings and how the artists created them. If I were to go alone, nobody would be around to disturb me.

Sample Answer 2

Go with a Group of People

1 **sociable person**
 - enjoy large groups
 - art galleries = not interesting → talk to people I go with

2 **more people = higher chance of clever observation**
 - can make good comment on artwork
 - make me realize new or interesting thought

Sample Response

Given the three choices regarding visiting an art gallery, I would select the third option and go with a group of people with varying levels of interest in art. The first reason I'd do that is that I'm a sociable person and always enjoy being in large groups. For me, art galleries aren't particularly interesting, so visiting one with several people would give me the opportunity to talk to them, which would make the trip better. The second reason is that if there are more people, the chances of someone making a clever or creative observation regarding the artwork will increase. In doing so, that person might make me realize something new or interesting about the art being discussed.

Question 2 p. 100

Listening Script

Now listen to two students discussing the announcement.

M Student: Jessica, you're planning on studying in Greece next semester, right?

W Student: That's right. I was accepted to a program in Athens, so I'll be gone the entire spring semester.

M: Did you see that financial aid is available for some students now?

W: Really?

M: Check out this announcement . . . So, uh, what do you think?

W: This is some of the best news I've heard in a long time. I'm so pleased the school will give students money to study abroad. My parents are concerned about how we're going to pay for everything. If I win a scholarship, it will be tremendously helpful.

M: Well, personally, I think the school should spend money only on students studying on campus.

W: I disagree with you.

M: Why do you say that?

W: The point of attending college is to have new learning experiences, and studying abroad can teach students countless lessons. My friends who studied abroad all told me it was one of their best semesters at school. In my opinion, more students should consider studying elsewhere for at least one semester.

Sample Answer

Reading Note

Juniors & seniors can get scholarships

- up to half off tuition to study abroad
- depends on grades and need

Listening Note

Woman → likes decision

1 **parents concerned about cost**
   - win scholarship = helpful

2 **new experiences at college**
   - studying abroad → learn many lessons
   - friends said was one of best semesters at school

Sample Response

The woman and the man have a conversation about an announcement made by the university study abroad office. The announcement mentions that sixty sophomores and juniors who study abroad can have up to half of their tuition paid for if they win a scholarship. The woman expresses her pleasure upon hearing about the announcement. The first reason she supports this decision by the university is that she and her parents are concerned about the cost of studying abroad. She intends to study in Greece for one semester but isn't sure how she can afford it. Winning a scholarship would help her very much. The second reason she gives is that her friends who studied abroad have mentioned how educational the experience was. She believes all students should study abroad at some point in their lives. So having the school pay for a part of that experience would benefit many people.

Question 3

p. 101

Listening Script

Now listen to a lecture on this topic in a psychology class.

M Professor: One problem some people have is that they refuse to consider other viewpoints. Instead, they get so involved in their own beliefs that they disregard other legitimate arguments, many of which are stronger than theirs.

Let me give you two personal examples. A few years ago, I assigned my class a term paper on alternative energy. They had to come up with both positive and negative features of it and speak with me about their thoughts before writing. One student told me she wanted to write about how horrible and harmful solar energy is. I'm not sure why, but she had nothing positive to say about it and only focused on its negative aspects. I tried to convince her otherwise, but her tunnel vision prevented her from seeing any.

I've also been guilty of tunnel vision. Years ago, I worked as a policeman. I was investigating a robbery and was positive I knew who had committed the crime. This man had an extensive criminal record, including theft, and I focused only on him. My partner wanted to investigate other suspects, but I disregarded him. As it turned out, that man was innocent, and we found the real thief. But due to my reluctance to consider other options, it took us several months to make an arrest.

Sample Answer

Reading Note

1 **tunnel vision = loss of peripheral vision**
   - can't see objects to either side
   - focus on what is straight ahead

2 **tunnel vision in psychology**
   - can't consider alternative viewpoints
   - only accept own opinions
   - believe in stereotypes

Listening Note

1 **assigned term paper**
   - think of positive and negative features
   - student only thought of negative ones
   - nothing positive to say

2 **prof was policeman**
   - investigate robbery → thought he knew criminal
   - only investigated that man
   - man was innocent → took months to find real thief

Sample Response

The professor talks about a couple of incidents related to his jobs as a teacher and a policeman. One time while teaching, he told his students to talk to him about their ideas for writing a paper describing positive and negative characteristics of alternative energy before beginning. One student wanted to focus only on the negative aspects of solar energy. Because she had tunnel vision, she refused to listen to the professor discuss some of its positive features. In addition, when the professor was a policeman, he thought he knew the identity of a criminal in a robbery case. He ignored his partner, who wanted to investigate other suspects, and only looked at one man. It turned out that the professor had been wrong. Both incidents are examples of tunnel vision. This happens when people figuratively look straight ahead and fail to consider anything else around them, which restricts their thinking.

Question 4

Listen to part of a lecture in an environmental science class.

M Professor: It's common for people to complain about pollution. Air pollution caused by smog, ground pollution caused by litter, and water pollution caused by oil spills are all common topics. Right now, I'd like to cover a fourth type of pollution, uh, which doesn't get as much publicity as the others. I'm speaking, of course, about noise pollution.

It's a shame more people don't think much about noise pollution because it can be quite harmful to humans. For instance, a recent study indicated that constant exposure to noise fifty-five decibels or higher can have harmful effects on people. Just so you know, that's a bit louder than the noise made by light traffic on city streets, so it's not terribly loud. Anyway, studies show that people exposed to constant noise this level or higher are more likely to suffer from cardiovascular problems. These include high blood pressure, heart attacks, and heart disease. It's estimated that millions of people have had their lives shortened due to noise pollution.

Noise pollution can also have deleterious effects on young people. As you know, we're located beneath a flight path for airplanes taking off and landing at the local airport. What happens every time a plane passes by . . . ? Yeah, everyone looks up, so your studies are disturbed. The teacher also stops talking momentarily because of the loud noise. Studies show that students exposed to excessive noise like this have lower reading skills than students at schools with low noise levels. Students exposed to loud noise also suffer from higher levels of stress, become angry easily, and are impatient. Clearly, um, something needs to be done to counter noise pollution.

Listening Note
Noise Pollution

1 **noise pollution = harms humans**
   - 55+ decibels → harmful
   - people exposed to constant noise = cardiovascular problems
   - millions have lives shortened

2 **noise from airport + planes**
   - studies interrupted by noise
   - students → lower reading skills
   - students have lots of stress, get angry, and impatient

The professor lectures to the class about noise pollution, which is a kind of pollution that he says many people don't think about. He points out that noise pollution can be very harmful to people. For instance, he remarks that if people are constantly exposed to noise that is fifty-five decibels or higher, then they are likely to have cardiovascular problems. He stresses that this level of noise is just a bit louder than light traffic on the streets. And he notes that it can cause people to have heart attacks, high blood pressure, and other heart problems. The professor then gives another negative effect of noise pollution. He says that when planes fly over the classroom, students and teachers both stop what they're doing. Exposure to loud noises like airplanes can lower students' reading abilities, make them get angry easily, and cause a lot of stress for them.

Actual Test 17

Question 1

Watching Videos

1 **advantages**
   - view videos again & again → reinforce learning
   - watched vids on Greece many times → know a lot about time period
   - videos use visual effects → good learning tool for me

2 **disadvantages**
   - can't ask questions → sit passively
   - some videos = biased
   - omit important information → propaganda

Sample Response

Watching videos as a way to learn has a couple of advantages. One is that you can view the videos again and again, which can help reinforce your learning. I have several videos on ancient Greece which I have watched multiple times. Thanks to them, I know quite a lot about that period in history. Another advantage is that videos rely on visual effects. I learn well when I see pictures, so videos are ideal learning tools for me. As for the disadvantages, you can't ask any questions when you're watching a video. You merely sit passively and take in the information. In addition, some videos are biased and omit important information because their creators aren't interested in the truth. Instead, their goal is to make propaganda.

Sample Answer 2

Taking Classes with Teachers

1 **advantages**
   - teachers ask questions → go back over information
   - discuss topics related to material → classes = more interesting

2 **disadvantages**
   - teachers uninterested in teaching → students learn little
   - teachers treat students poorly → mean + play favorites

Sample Response

Taking classes with teachers has both advantages and disadvantages. Let me cover the advantages first. Teachers frequently ask students questions to test if they are learning. If students answer incorrectly, teachers can go back over the information until the students know it. In addition, students can ask teachers to discuss topics related to the material in their classes. That makes classes more interesting. However, there are also disadvantages. I have had many teachers who are simply uninterested in passing on knowledge to students. I therefore learned little in their classes. Some teachers also treat their students poorly. They can be mean to some and play favorites with others. When they act that way, students aren't able to learn well in their classes.

Question 2

p. 106

Listening Script

Now listen to two students discussing the notice.

W Student: Oh, wow, this is a big move by the library.

M Student: You're talking about people being able to check out reference material from the library now, aren't you?

W: Yeah. I don't ever believe I've heard of a library doing something like this before. What do you think about this decision, Keith?

M: Hmm . . . That's a good question. On the one hand, I'll personally benefit because there are tons of reference books which I need to use. Instead of paying lots of money to make photocopies in the library, I'll be able to take the books home and scan important pages onto my computer. That will enable me to save money.

W: That's interesting. I had never considered that.

M: But there's also a negative side.

W: There is?

M: Sure. Imagine that you really need some information in a reference book for an assignment due the next day, but the book is checked out.

W: Oh . . . yeah.

M: That would be extremely unfortunate. So there's definitely a downside to this decision as well.

Sample Answer

Reading Note

Can check out reference books from library

- check out for 2 days
- no renewals
- pay for damage or lost book

Listening Note

Man → mixed feelings

1 **will benefit by saving money**
   - doesn't have to make copies in library
   - can scan books onto computer at home

2 **could have downside**
   - may need information in book for project due next day
   - but book is checked out

Sample Response

The two speakers are discussing a decision made by the university library. In the notice they read, it's mentioned that students, faculty, and staff members may now check out reference books. They won't be able to renew the books, and they are only allowed to borrow the material for two days at a time though. The man has mixed feelings about this decision by the library. To begin with, he supports the decision because he will benefit financially. Instead of paying money to photocopy pages of material in the library, he can borrow reference books, take them home, and scan important pages onto his computer. However, he dislikes the decision because he's concerned about other people checking out reference material he may need. He points out that he would have a problem if he needed a book for an assignment due the next day but discovered that it had been checked out.

Question 3

p. 107

Listening Script

Now listen to a lecture on this topic in a marketing class.

M Professor: Of all the different types of marketing campaigns employed today, arguably the one focusing the most on the long term is relationship marketing. Businesses have devised numerous ways to improve their relationships with their customers.

Let me see . . . A few years ago, my family and I went to the beach for a vacation. When we arrived at the hotel, the desk clerk asked if I was a member of the hotel's members-only club. I responded no and inquired about the benefits. It turns out that by becoming a member, I could receive a twenty-percent discount anytime I stayed there. Since it's a chain with hotels around the country, I signed up immediately. I love traveling, and I also love saving money, so it was a great deal.

We stayed there for two weeks, and during that time, my wife celebrated her birthday. Well, on the morning of her birthday, a member of the hotel staff visited our room and wished her a happy birthday. Then, he provided my wife with a voucher that she could use for a free dinner at the hotel's restaurant. Finally, she was given a complimentary birthday cake. That was the best service I've ever gotten, and I've been sure to stay at that hotel every opportunity I get.

Sample Answer

Reading Note

Modern marketing campaigns

think of negative things that could happen

- retain customers + develop long-term relationships
- provide outstanding services and products
- provide perks → encourage customers to have continuous dealings

Listening Note

1 **went on vacation**
   - joined hotel's members-only club
   - 20% discount → signed up

2 **two-week vacation**
   - wife had birthday
   - wished happy birthday by staff
   - got voucher for free meal + cake

Sample Response

During his lecture, the professor tells the class about a trip he took a few years ago. He mentions that a hotel clerk invited him to join its members-only club, and he agreed when he discovered he could get a big discount. He points out that he stays at that hotel a lot when he travels since it's a nationwide chain. The professor also states that while at the hotel, his wife celebrated her birthday. A hotel staffer wished his wife a happy birthday, and she was given a voucher for a free meal as well as a free cake. The professor was extremely pleased with the service he received at the hotel. The actions at the hotel are related to relationship marketing. It is used by businesses to establish long-term relationships with customers. By offering perks or providing excellent service, businesses can get the most out of their relationships with customers.

Question 4

p. 108

Listening Script

Listen to part of a lecture in an archaeology class.

W Professor: The ruins which I just showed you are from an agricultural site in Egypt. They're more than 4,000 years old. Impressive, huh? You know, uh, agriculture was discovered around 10,000 years ago, and humans then had to come up with ways to water their crops. Some of the methods they devised were quite clever.

Here's a picture of the method used in ancient Egypt . . . This was known as basin irrigation. Basically, the Egyptians relied on the Nile River, which flooded annually, to water their crops. Their fields were basins which had low walls surrounding them. Whenever it was time to water their crops, they broke holes in the walls to their fields, and water that they had captured from the Nile floods entered. As soon as enough water got in, floodgates were opened so that water was then diverted to even more fields. This farming method was quite effective, but one drawback was that the Egyptians were only able to harvest crops once a year.

The Mesopotamians in the Middle East came up with a different method of irrigating their fields, and it was one that permitted them an extensive growing season, so their farmers could grow two or more crops a year. The Mesopotamian method was called perennial irrigation. The Tigris and Euphrates rivers ran through the region there, so the Mesopotamians constructed various channels, waterways, and canals connected to the rivers and leading to their fields. This let them control the flow of water all year long. This became a very popular method of irrigation and was adopted for use in places such as China and India in ancient times.

Listening Note

Ancient Irrigation Methods

1 **basin irrigation**
   - used by Egyptians
   - fields = basins w/low walls
   - broke holes in walls → let water in
   - floodgates sent water to other fields
   - harvested 1 crop/year

2 **perennial irrigation**
   - used by Mesopotamians
   - made waterways connecting rivers to fields
   - controlled flow of water all year
   - grew 2+ crops/year

Sample Response

The professor tells the class that some of the irrigation methods used in ancient times were clever, and he cites examples from ancient Egypt and Mesopotamia as proof. The first example, from Egypt, is called basin irrigation. The professor mentions that the Egyptians captured water from the Nile River when it flooded every year. They had fields in basins which were surrounded by walls. When the crops needed water, they poked holes in the walls, and floodwater rushed in. Then, they used floodgates to let water get into more fields. This method let the Egyptians get one crop annually. As for the Mesopotamians, they used perennial irrigation. They built canals and other waterways that went from the Tigris and Euphrates rivers to their fields. Since the waterways connected to the rivers, they could obtain water all year long. This allowed them to raise multiple crops every year.

Actual Test 18

Question 1
p. 111

Sample Answer 1

Allow Children to Watch Any Programs

1 **children make good choices**
   - sis and I watched cartoons
   - harmless and educational

2 **can discover fun and interesting programs**
   - changed channels → watched documentaries
   - learned about animals, places, and people

Sample Response

Of the two choices, the former is much more appealing to me. I think parents should allow their children to watch any programs they are interested in. First of all, most children make good choices regarding the programs they watch. For instance, when my sister and I were younger, we mostly watched cartoons. Those were harmless yet also educated us in some ways. Secondly, if children can choose what they watch, they might discover some fun and interesting programs. My sister and I often changed the channels when we were bored. Whenever we saw documentaries, we usually watched them. So we learned about all kinds of animals, places, and people because our parents let us make our own viewing choices when we were watching television.

Sample Answer 2

Monitor Children's Viewing

1 **many bad shows**
   - exposed kids to violence, bad language, and nudity
   - parents monitored my watching → wasn't exposed to bad things

2 **cartoons can be harmful**
   - have political agendas + propaganda
   - parents banned from watching shows promoting bad lifestyles and activities

Sample Response

In this day and age, parents absolutely must monitor their children and only allow them to watch preapproved television programs. For starters, there are too many shows these days that contain violence, bad language, nudity, and other things children shouldn't be exposed to. Fortunately for me, my parents told me what I could and couldn't watch, so I wasn't exposed to anything negative when I was young. Additionally, even cartoons can be harmful to kids these days. A large number of them have political agendas and basically act as propaganda. My parents always banned me from watching certain shows because they promoted lifestyles and activities that my parents disagreed with. Personally, I'm glad they did that.

Question 2
p. 112

Listening Script

Now listen to two students discussing the announcement.

M Student: I'm hungry, Beth. Let's go to have lunch at Minter Dining Hall.

W Student: Um . . . Are we having lunch with a professor? Isn't that the only way we can get into that cafeteria?

M: Not anymore. The rules changed.

W: Seriously?

M: Totally. I can't wait to go there. I dined there with Professor Jackson once. The food was much better than at any of the other dining halls on campus. Honestly, uh, I don't mind the higher prices considering how delicious the meals are.

W: Are professors still going to dine there?

M: Yes, they are. And that's another reason I want to go.

W: Why is that?

M: I'd like to get to know some professors here on campus better. I might just ask a professor or two if I can sit next to them sometimes. If I talked to them while eating, I might learn something. For example, um, it would be great to have meals with some professors in my department.

W: That sounds good.

Sample Answer

Reading Note

Anyone can dine in faculty dining hall now

- only faculty and guests allowed before
- rule changed due to lobbying
- meals 50% higher than at other places

Listening Note

Man → approves of changes

1 **dined there once**
   - excellent food
   - doesn't mind high prices

2 **wants to eat w/professors**
   - will ask to sit w/them
   - if talk, can learn something

Sample Response

In their conversation, the two speakers talk about a change that is being made by the student dining services office. Starting on October 1, Minter Dining Hall, which has previously been open only to faculty members, will start permitting anyone to eat there. The man fully supports this decision and gives two reasons for having that opinion. The first is that he loves the taste of the food there. He mentions having eaten with a professor there once in the past, and he points out that the food in Minter Dining Hall was much better than at the school's other cafeterias. He doesn't even mind paying higher prices for better food. Another reason he gives is that he wants to meet some professors while eating there. The man believes that he can learn from them if he eats and has conversations with them at the same time.

Question 3

p. 113

Listening Script

Now listen to a lecture on this topic in an economics class.

W Professor: Now, uh, we read about the free-rider effect, but I want to give you some examples to clarify everything. You often see this happen with regard to government services, so those are the first two examples I'll cite.

Our city recently upgraded its major roads with a two-year construction project that cost tens of millions of dollars. Do you know where the money came from . . . ? It came from people like you and me, city residents who pay taxes. We contributed to the general welfare of the city's roads, but what about people from other cities who visit to go shopping at the mall or to use our recreational facilities? They're free riders because they're benefiting from the improvements made to the roads but paid absolutely nothing.

Here's another one . . . A decade ago, the city opened a popular museum of natural history. One of the best parts for many people was the lack of an admission fee. The museum was financed completely by donations from private individuals. Unfortunately, there were too many free riders who constantly used the facilities but contributed no money. The museum closed down three years ago because it couldn't support itself financially, and no big donors were willing to pay for something that would benefit lots of people unwilling to make even small contributions.

Sample Answer

Reading Note

Goods or services provided by one but used by others

think of negative things that could happen

- others = free riders
- benefit from actions of others
- contribute little or nothing themselves

Listening Note

1 **city upgraded major roads**
   - residents paid for upgrades through taxes
   - visitors to city didn't pay taxes = free riders
   - benefit from improvements but paid nothing

2 **city opened museum**
   - no admission fee → financed by donations
   - free riders used facilities but didn't donate
   - museum closed down → couldn't support self financially

During her lecture, the professor discusses a project by the city to improve the condition of its roads. She states that city taxpayers were responsible for paying for these upgrades, which cost millions of dollars. However, other people who use the roads, such as individuals from out of town coming to shop or to use recreational facilities, paid nothing yet benefit from the use of the roads. Then, the professor talks about a museum in the city. The only financing it received was from donations since it didn't charge admission. The museum had to close down because it didn't get enough money even though plenty of people visited it. In both cases, the free-rider effect can be seen. This refers to a situation where a person, company, or government provides or pays for resources, goods, or services while other people use them despite paying little or no money. These free riders benefit at almost no cost to themselves.

Question 4   p. 114

Listening Script

Listen to part of a lecture in an urban development class.

W Professor: Today's urban areas are often referred to as concrete jungles due to the large number of high-rise buildings found in them. In an effort to improve the standard of living in large metropolises, city planners strive to create green spaces such as parks. Because of a lack of space in most cities, urban planners have had to be creative with their methods. One such development is the linear park.

A linear park is a park that's much longer than it is wide. Waterfront linear parks are one type that has gained popularity in recent years. These parks typically run alongside a river running through a city. The Eastbank Esplanade in Portland, Oregon, is one such example. It extends nearly 2.5 kilometers by the Willamette River. It connects several neighborhoods and is used by pedestrians, cyclists, skateboarders, and others. Waterfront linear parks are typically used for recreation and can also be used by people doing water-related activities, including, uh, swimming, fishing, boating, and water-skiing.

Take a look at this picture . . . This is an elevated linear park. Personally, I find this kind of park to be the most creative. Elevated linear parks are constructed above the ground by using places such as abandoned highways and railways. In Manhattan in New York City, the High Line is an elevated linear park. It runs aboveground for approximately 2.3 kilometers and is built on an old rail line. The park has lots of plants growing in it, and they attract birds and butterflies. There are even art exhibits and other cultural events held there, which can help people forget they're in the middle of an overpopulated city.

Sample Answer

Listening Note
Linear Parks

1 **waterfront linear parks**
   - along rivers in cities
   - Eastbank Esplanade → connects neighborhoods in Portland
   - used for recreation + water-related activities

2 **elevated linear parks**
   - above ground on abandoned highways and railways
   - High Line in Manhattan → built on rail line
   - has plants, birds, and butterflies
   - has art exhibits + cultural events

Sample Response

The professor lectures to the students about linear parks, which she says are parks that are longer than they are wide and are often used by city planners to add green spaces to crowded cities. In her talk, she discusses waterfront linear parks and elevated linear parks. Regarding waterfront linear parks, she points out that they are typically built next to a river that flows through a city. She mentions the Eastbank Esplanade, a linear park in Portland, Oregon, as an example. Cyclists, pedestrians, and others use it as they move through different neighborhoods. She also comments that people do water-related activities like swimming and fishing in waterside linear parks. As for elevated linear parks, they are built aboveground on old roads or railways. The High Line in Manhattan is one such park. It has plenty of trees and wildlife, and it even hosts art exhibits and cultural events.

Actual Test 19

Question 1   p. 117

Sample Answer 1

Excellent Professors and Facilities but High Tuition

1 **attend school to learn**
   - can get great education
   - easy to get good job + be successful

2 **okay to pay high tuition**
   - find part-time job + take out loans
   - bro attended expensive college → had job + got loans
     = successful today

In my opinion, the choice is a simple one. I would opt to attend the expensive school with topnotch professors and facilities. First, the primary reason to attend school is to learn. If my school has the best professors and facilities, then I'll be able to get a great education. That means it should be easy for me to acquire a good job and to be successful. Second, although my family isn't wealthy, I don't mind paying high tuition. I can find a part-time job, and I can also take out loans to pay my tuition. My older brother attended an expensive college, and that's exactly what he did. He told me it was difficult, but he doesn't regret anything, especially since he's extremely successful in his profession today.

Sample Answer 2

Average Professors and Facilities but Free to Attend

1 family doesn't have much money
- free school = appealing
- cousin attended expensive school 10 years ago → still paying off loans

2 can still get quality education
- study hard and do best
- father didn't attend good school but got good education
- studied hard and tried in all classes

I would love to attend a school with outstanding professors and facilities, but I would select the second choice. The main reason is that my family doesn't have much money, so attending a university for free is very appealing. My cousin went to an expensive school, and, ten years after graduating, she's still repaying the loans she took out to pay her tuition. I don't want to be burdened like that. In addition, even if the professors and facilities are average, I can still obtain a quality education by studying hard and by doing my best. My father didn't attend a good school, but he's still highly educated. The reason is that he constantly studied at school and tried hard in every class he took.

Question 2

p. 118

Listening Script

Now listen to two students discussing the notice.

W Student: Well, this is cool. There will be single rooms in some dorms next semester.

M Student: I saw that. Will you apply for one?

W: I'm not sure yet since I can see both positive and negative aspects.

M: I have my own thoughts but would love to hear yours, too.

W: Obviously, the cost is pretty high. I mean, that's the main reason I'm not extremely excited. The price of a single room will be about $2,000 extra each semester. That's a lot, and I don't know if I can pay that.

M: That's the main disadvantage for me. I don't have enough money for a single.

W: I'm sorry to hear that.

M: So, uh, what's something positive?

W: That's easy. I'm going to be ridiculously busy during my senior year. I'll be taking three seminars as well as some lab classes. I'll be staying up late almost every night as well, so if I don't have a roommate, it'll be easy for me to, uh, to study in my room.

M: Good point. I mainly want a single because I dislike sharing a room with someone else.

Sample Answer

Reading Note

Juniors & seniors can have single dorm rooms
- 250 single rooms
- sign up for lottery to determine who gets room
- price of room is 2x higher than double room

Listening Note

Woman → mixed feelings

1 high cost
- $2,000 extra/semester
- doesn't think can pay that

2 will be easy to study in room
- senior year = very busy
- will stay up late studying every night

The woman and the man discuss a notice issued by the university student housing office. A decision has been made to let some students stay in rooms by themselves in the school's dormitories. 250 students will get singles that will be more expensive than regular rooms. The woman has mixed feelings about the change in policy. She's worried about the expense as she points out that a single will cost $2,000 more per semester than a regular dorm room. She remarks that the price may be too much for her. On the other hand, she likes the idea of staying in a single room because she's going to be busy during her senior year. She points out that due to the classes she is taking, she will have to stay up late studying most nights. If she has a single, that will be easy for her to do.

Question 3

p. 119

Listening Script

Now listen to a lecture on this topic in a psychology class.

M Professor: It's natural for us to look around, to see how others are doing, and then to, um, to make comparisons in our own lives. Everybody does that. I definitely do, and I'm sure all of you do that as well. Interestingly, there can be both positive and negative results of making these comparisons.

One of my college roommates was extremely competitive. He was always comparing himself to others, particularly those doing better than him. He was a good baseball player, but he wanted to become better. He compared himself to professional ballplayers by imitating their styles and their work habits. Guess what . . . It worked. He became a professional baseball player and even made the all-star team a couple of times. He's a retired millionaire today.

On the other hand, another one of my old college friends had some negative results from his use of upward comparison. He came from a lower-class family, and he really envied the upper-class lifestyle. He tried living it but didn't have enough money. He maxed out his credit cards and borrowed lots of money from friends while trying to hang out with his wealthy buddies. Sadly, he accrued a tremendous amount of debt and has had financial problems ever since college.

Sample Answer

Reading Note

1 **people make comparisons between selves and others**
   - compare w/those better off
   - determine how to improve lives

2 **negative effects**
   - feelings of envy or jealousy
   - see others more successful

Listening Note

1 **roommate = competitive**
   - compared self to others
   - imitated styles and habits of pro ballplayers
   - became pro → retired as millionaire

2 **college friend = negative results**
   - envied upper-class lifestyle
   - didn't have enough money → borrowed + used credit cards
   - lots of debts + financial problems

Sample Response

While lecturing on upward comparison, the professor tells the class about two people he knew from college. The first person he discusses is his college roommate. He wanted to become the best professional baseball player, so he looked at pro ballplayers and imitated them in various ways. He managed to become an all-star player and retired a rich man. On the other hand, another of the professor's friends had a negative experience. He wanted to live like his upper-class friends, so he borrowed money and used his credit cards. Because he envied their lifestyles, he acquired a lot of debt. Both people made upward comparisons which affected their lives. This happens when people compare their lives to those more successful than them and try to imitate those individuals. There can be positive results, like the roommate, or negative results, like the professor's friend, when upward comparisons are made.

Question 4

p. 120

Listening Script

Listen to part of a lecture in an ecology class.

M Professor: The Pampas is a lowland area in South America in parts of Brazil and Argentina and all of Uruguay. Much of the Pampas consists of grasslands. These areas have temperate climates and receive moderate amounts of rainfall, making for very fertile land. Yet they are quite windy and endure a dry season, too. Due to the ecosystem there, some plants grow especially well in the Pampas grasslands.

The first is the aptly named Pampas grass, a hearty type of grass which can grow in both dry and moist soil. Interestingly, unlike regular grass, some species of Pampas grass can grow up to nearly four meters in height despite having leaves only one or two centimeters wide. It grows in large clumps and has leaves as sharp as razors. One unique feature of Pampas grass is its enormous root system that descends deep underground. When annual fires rage through the grasslands, the leaves get burned, but the plant grows again soon afterward because its root system remains intact.

Another common Pampas grassland plant is the ombu. Spell that O-M-B-U. The ombu is actually a bush; however, it can have a trunk with a diameter of fifteen meters and can grow to be nearly twenty meters high. The ombu thrives in areas where Pampas grasslands are dry because it doesn't need much water to survive. It also has poisonous sap, so herbivores don't eat its leaves, and it's highly resistant to fire, too. As a result, while wildfires burn most trees in the Pampas grasslands, the ombu survives. And on the rare occasions that an ombu does burn, its strong root system lets it grow back even faster than before.

Listening Note

Pampas Grassland Plants

1 Pampas = lowland area in S. America
- temperate climate + moderate rainfall = fertile
- some plants grow well there

2 Pampas grass
- grows 4m high w/razor-sharp leaves
- root system deep underground
- fires burn plants + root system intact → plant grows again

3 ombu
- bush w/trunk w/15m diameter + 20m high
- grows in dry land since needs little water
- resistant to fire → wildfires don't burn down
- if burns, root system lets grow back fast

During his lecture, the professor talks about Pampas grass and the ombu, two plants which thrive in the Pampas grasslands. The Pampas is an area in South America in Argentina, Uruguay, and Brazil. Its temperate climate and moderate rainfall, along with a dry season, give it fertile land. One plant that does well there is Pampas grass, which can have leaves nearly four meters high. Pampas grass has a root system that goes deep beneath the ground, so when the annual fires come and burn the leaves of the grass, the plant doesn't die. Instead, thanks to its roots, it grows again soon. The ombu is another Pampas grassland plant. It's a bush that looks like a tree since it can grow around twenty meters high. The ombu does well in dry grasslands since it needs little water to survive. It's also fire resistant, so it can survive wildfires whereas most trees there get burned.

Actual Test 20

Question 1
p. 123

All Members of the Public

1 local residents have shared history
- should be able to explore
- learn about it firsthand

2 support site financially
- help preserve site for research
- nearby historical site → popular place in city

It would be so exciting if an area of historical interest were discovered in my local area. As a result, I believe every member of the public who is willing to pay an admission fee should be allowed to visit it. One reason I feel this way is that the people in an area have a shared history. Thus they should all be permitted to explore it and to learn about it firsthand. In addition, by paying an admission fee, visitors would be supporting the site financially. This would enable it to be preserved and to have research done on it. There is an historical site nearby which allows visitors, and it's one of my city's most popular places. I wish there were more places like it.

Only Experts Working to Preserve the Site

1 experts know how to act
- won't destroy valuable items or cause problems
- visitor at historical home sat on old chair and broke it → expert wouldn't do

2 preserve site for future
- uncle is archaeologist → has worked on many sites
- preserves sites and artifacts for future generations

I strongly feel that only experts who are working to help preserve the site should be permitted access to it. One of the reasons is that experts know how to act when they're working at historical sites. So they won't destroy anything valuable or cause any problems. Just last month, a visitor at a local historical home sat in a 200-year-old chair and broke it. An expert would never do anything like that. In addition, experts should be allowed to preserve the site so that it can be enjoyed and studied in the future. My uncle is an archaeologist who has worked on many dig sites. Thanks to him and others like him, important places and artifacts have been preserved for future generations.

Question 2
p. 124

Now listen to two students discussing the announcement.

W Student: I didn't realize we were getting a new law school in a few years. That's surprising.

M Student: It is, but I can't believe where the university intends to put it.

W: Why is that? Is something wrong?

M: There's actually a huge problem. That area is a wetland which should be protected, not developed.

W: What do you mean?

M: Haven't you ever wondered why there are so many birds around campus? Large numbers of migratory birds, particularly waterfowl, live in that area. Some even lay their eggs there. If that land gets developed, thousands of birds will have their ecosystem destroyed.

W: Huh . . . I never realized that.

M: In addition, wetlands are effective at preventing flooding. The existence of that land is one reason the Trident River almost never floods. If the wetland disappears, we might get flooded at times during the rainstorms that happen in April and May.

W: Oh, my. That would be awful.

M: You're right about that. I'm going to talk to someone in the administration and file a complaint.

Sample Answer

Reading Note
University will develop land

- land next to river
- will put new law school there

Listening Note
Man → dislikes decision

1 **wetland should be protected**
   - migratory birds live there
   - if land developed, ecosystem for birds destroyed

2 **wetlands prevent flooding**
   - river rarely floods now
   - if no wetlands, could be floods during rainstorms

Sample Response

The speakers are having a conversation about the decision by the university development office to develop some land the school recently acquired. Apparently, the school will use the fifty acres of land it bought to construct a new law school. The man is strongly against this decision by the school, and he gives a couple of reasons for feeling that way. The first is that the land to be developed is a wetland used by migratory birds. He points out that birds have nests there and lay eggs in the wetland, so developing it could be harmful to many birds. The second reason the man gives is that developing the wetland could result in flooding. He mentions that wetlands are good at stopping floods, so he notes that if there are no more wetlands, when spring rains fall later, the university could suffer from some flooding.

Question 3
p. 125

Listening Script

Now listen to a lecture on this topic in a biology class.

W Professor: If you visit a forest, you'll be exposed to a natural environment. There, plants, animals, and other species coexist and form an ecosystem involving countless interactions between them. In addition, there are large numbers of artificial environments around the world.

One is the greenhouse. We use greenhouses to grow crops during times when or in places where they wouldn't normally grow. Greenhouses are used to control the amount of sunlight, the temperature, and the amount of water that plants are exposed to. There's absolutely nothing natural about them, but it's thanks to greenhouses that we can grow, uh, tomatoes and cabbage in wintertime and raise tropical fruits in places that get cold weather.

The farm is another example of an artificial environment. Think about what farmers do . . . They cut down trees, till fields, and plant crops in them. They make the soil more fertile by adding fertilizer to it. Everything they do changes the natural environment. Do you know what happens when farms are abandoned? Within a few years, they look entirely different. In some cases, entire forests grow on abandoned farms. Additionally, plants native to the region start growing again. If you look at before-and-after photos of farmland that reverts to nature, you'll be astonished by the changes from an artificial environment to a natural one.

Sample Answer

Reading Note
Artificial environment = made by humans

- don't exist in natural conditions
- lack of diversity in plants and animal life
- not sustainable w/out human intervention
- fall apart unless humans act

Listening Note

1 **greenhouses = grow crops when and where can't**
   - control sunlight, temperature, and water
   - can get fruits and vegetables in winter and cold places

2 **farm = artificial environment**
   - change area to grow crops
   - abandoned farms → change quickly
   - forests grow + native plants come back

Sample Response

The professor tells the students about some artificial environments and uses greenhouses and farms as examples. About greenhouses, she comments that everything about them, including the temperature and the amount of sunlight and water, is artificial. However, they are beneficial since they allow people to grow plants such as tomatoes, cabbage, and tropical fruits in conditions that are less than ideal. About farms, the professor points out that farmers completely change the natural environment by tilling the land, planting crops, and adding fertilizer. She then mentions that when farms are abandoned, nature quickly transforms them back to their natural environments. Both greenhouse and farms are artificial environments, which are ecosystems that don't form due to natural causes. They are not diverse with regard to plant and animal life, and they are also unsustainable when humans stop taking care of them. So they will return to their original state once humans leave them alone.

Question 4

p. 126

Listening Script

Listen to part of a lecture in an environmental science class.

W Professor: We all know solar panels have limitations. For example, they can only produce energy during daylight hours, and they're relatively inefficient, too. But there are other problems related to solar energy that have nothing to do with the panels themselves. These issues are particularly noticeable in urban centers.

Here's a picture of downtown London . . . And here's one of Chicago . . . and one of Toronto . . . Did you notice anything about the buildings? Well, uh, aside from the fact that they're tall, the buildings are all different sizes. Some are much higher than the buildings alongside them. This poses a major problem for a building with solar panels on its roof. If the roof is obstructed from sunlight due to the placement of another building, the building simply cannot use solar power at all. In other cases, buildings might block solar panels on other skyscrapers for a few hours a day. In doing so, their placement reduces the amount of solar energy those buildings can produce.

Another problem concerns the sizes of the buildings. One benefit of skyscrapers is that they're much higher than they are wide. Therefore, um, high-rise apartments and office buildings can hold hundreds or thousands of people yet not even take up an entire city block. But imagine if solar panels were put on the roof of one of those buildings— even an unobstructed one. Due to the enormous energy requirements of, uh, let's say, 1,000 people in the building, there's no way the solar panels could produce enough energy for everyone. So a skyscraper could reduce its reliance on fossil fuels, but it couldn't rely 100% on solar energy.

Listening Note

Solar Power

1 buildings in big cities different heights
- can obstruct solar panels on roof → not enough sunlight
- completely block or block for few hours → reduces amount of solar energy can produce

2 sizes of buildings
- skyscrapers = very tall → hundreds or thousands of people in them
- solar panels on roof can't support everyone in building
- can't rely 100% on solar energy

The professor's lecture is about some limitations that solar power has in urban centers. She points out that building placement and the sizes of buildings are two major issues concerning solar power. The first limitation she discusses concerns the placement of buildings. She shows some pictures and points out the different sizes of the buildings. She mentions that some buildings are completely obstructed from sunlight by others. As a result, they cannot have solar panels placed on their roofs. Other buildings might be obstructed for a few hours, so they cannot use solar panels to their full potential. The second topic, the sizes of buildings, concerns the fact that buildings are much higher than they are wide. This enables thousands of people to use buildings, which means they have tremendous energy needs. Solar panels on the roofs of these buildings cannot provide all of the energy they need in that case.

Memo

Memo